The psychology of the female body

Critical Psychology

Series editors

John Broughton
Columbia University

David Ingleby
Vakgroep Ontwikkeling en Socialisatie, Utrecht

Valerie Walkerdine
University of London Institute of Education

Since the 1960s there has been widespread disaffection with traditional approaches in psychology, and talk of a 'crisis' has been endemic. At the same time, psychology has encountered influential contemporary movements such as feminism, neo-marxism, post-structuralism, and post-modernism. In this climate, various forms of 'critical psychology' have developed vigorously.

Unfortunately, such work — drawing as it does on unfamiliar intellectual traditions — is often difficult to assimilate. The aim of the Critical Psychology series is to make this exciting new body of work readily accessible to students and teachers of psychology, as well as presenting the more psychological aspects of this work to a wider social scientific audience. Specially commissioned works from leading critical writers will demonstrate the relevance of their new approaches to a wide range of current social issues.

Titles in the series include

The Crisis in Modern Social Psychology
Ian Parker

The Psychology of the Female Body
Jane M. Ussher

Significant Differences
Corinne Squire

The psychology of the female body

Jane M. Ussher

ROUTLEDGE
London and New York

First published in 1989 by Routledge
11 New Fetter Lane, London EC4P 4EE
29 West 35th Street, New York NY 10001

Printed and bound in Great Britain by Biddles Ltd,
Guildford and King's Lynn
Typeset by Pat and Anne Murphy, Highcliffe-on-Sea, Dorset

British Library Cataloguing in Publication Data

Ussher, Jane M.
   The psychology of the female body.
   1. Women. Psychology
   I. Title
   155.6'33

Library of Congress Cataloging in Publication Data

Ussher, Jane M., 1961–
   The psychology of the female body.
   (Critical psychology series)
   Originally presented as the author's thesis (Ph.D.)
   Bibliography: p.
   Includes index.
   1. Women—Psychology. 2. Women—Physiology. 3. Body
image. I. Title. II. Series.
HQ1206.U84 1989   155.6'33   88-35678

ISBN 0-415-01556-1
ISBN 0-415-01557-X (pbk.)

For Christopher Dewberry

Contents

Preface

At this point I would like to clarify my own position in this debate and my purpose in this book. I first became interested in the psychology of the female body and reproduction as a worthy topic of study for a PhD thesis. It seemed important to me, as a fledgling postgraduate, to design straightforward quantitative experiments which would provide some scientific 'truth' regarding the possible influences of the cyclicity of menstruation on women. Following the idealism of many postgraduates before me, I had the misconception that all I had to do was design the perfect experiment and all would be revealed. It was a long time before it dawned on me that there was far more to the issue of cyclicity and reproduction than could ever be contained in any research experiment. I became aware of the myriad issues and questions never addressed by psychologists, who appeared to believe that a simple causal relationship could be found between, for example, one aspect of personality and menstrual-cycle distress, and thus largely explain the influence of menstruation on behaviour.

I could now see the limitations of empiricism: 'the unsystematic registration of things as they are and the refusal of forms of analysis which penetrate beneath the surface of observable social phenomena' (Rose 1986: 26). My previous naivety astounded me, as did psychology's positivistic approach to a complicated aspect of women's experience. Questions which seemed to be of relevance and importance, such as why women's reproductive experiences are invariably understood in terms of an illness model, or why there was such a strong perpetuation of the archetype of the unreliable menstruating woman — despite evidence to the contrary — seemed to be of much greater importance and interest than those questions to which I had originally addressed myself.

Yet to achieve the PhD I continued to pursue the half-formed research questions: analysing the relationship between physiological state, cognitive performance, and mood change in an experimental setting with a small group of women. My quantitative results were all negative, suggesting little evidence of cyclicity. So, having gained the qualification I had striven and compromised for, I found myself presenting my findings at conferences in support of my argument that there was little or no validity in the biological theories, and that psychology should get away altogether from its hormonal syndrome approach to women's behaviour.

Paradoxically, in order to support the view that there is no basis in the biologically deterministic arguments which see woman ruled by her womb, I have found myself turning to those very experiments whose theoretical premises I also criticize. In a wider analytical context such quantitative empirical studies can be useful and we certainly cannot ignore them. Whatever our criticisms of their foundations (such as those of Kitzinger 1987), they provide the basis for many claims about women's bodies and need to be examined in this light.

Within this book I try to present a wider analysis of the psychology of the female body than that usually considered by psychologists. It is the perpetuation of this biologically reductive account of women in contemporary psychology which has led me to write this book, which is intended for both psychologists and those with a more general interest in the psychology of women and the female body (and reproduction) in particular. It is also intended for women who have an interest in how the female body has been conceptualized and used against us by the scientific experts, and who seek an alternative perspective. I hope I have made it accessible to these different audiences. Thus it is not merely a discussion of the many research studies carried out in this area accompanied by a methodical criticism of each. It is also meant as an overview of the way in which women's bodies and our reproductive cycles have been understood and explained, and of the contribution which these explanations make to women's identity.

My analysis is primarily based on the experiences of women in the West and cannot automatically be applied to women from other cultures or other points in history; our understanding of the female body is too bound up with cultural practices for that. It may well be possible to extrapolate from some parts of this study to women in other cultures but I restrict discussion to the Western world out of respect for different cultural practices, which I do not pretend fully to understand.

I have written this book because of a belief that there is a need to link together our understanding of the different — and, at present, fragmented — aspects of women's experience associated with our bodies, particularly surrounding menstruation, pregnancy and the menopause, and to show that this is a valid area of study for psychologists. It is not a fringe issue, as some might suggest, only of interest to a few obscure women researchers (such as myself!). It is important to anyone who is attempting to understand the experience of women.

It is vital that an alternative viewpoint to the 'raging-hormones' theory is advocated and argued, so that women can see that biologically reductive explanations for their experiences are insufficient. I am not going to propose numerous interventions to cope with the distress and problems associated with our bodies which women experience, but I hope to pull together some of the many threads of the experience of having a female body, so that as women we may make choices about our needs whilst putting our experiences in context. At present, many of women's experiences associated with the female body, and with reproduction in particular, are fragmented and dislocated, seen as separate entities, separate life phases, with little common ground. I want to show that this is not only incorrect but potentially damaging for women, as it acts to fragment the self, as well as perpetuating the pathologizing of behaviour.

Acknowledgements

Thanks to Valerie Walkerdine for the most thorough editorial advice, as well as encouragement. John Wilding, who supervised my PhD, provided both supportive and constructive supervision, enabling me to finish the research and thus write this book.

To all the women I talked to when carrying out the research, as well as those who underwent hours of tedious experiments, I am most grateful.

Finally, thanks go to my mother Elizabeth Ussher, for providing me with a model of hard work which has sustained me throughout the writing of this book.

Chapter 1

Framing women — anatomy as destiny

the affective life is more developed in proportion to the intellect in the female than in the male sex, and the influence of the reproductive organs upon the mind more powerful.

anatomy is destiny . . . insofar as it determines not only the range and configuration of physiological functioning and its limitation, but also, to an extent, personality configurations. The basic commitment and involvement naturally also reflect the groundplan of the body.

(Erikson 1968: 337)

Biological difference and nature, specifically the capacity of women to reproduce, has been used for centuries in almost all societies to justify the subjugation of women. Women have been conceptualized as being ruled by their bodies, bodies which are seen as unstable and inherently weak. Traditionally, biology has been put forward as a justification for excluding women from education or the workforce, and the biological argument was taken on uncritically by the early psychologists. Maudsley (1874) and Spencer (1896) were typical in arguing against the growth in women's higher education in Britain and America, because of the potential 'diminution of reproductive power' (Spencer 1896) which might occur, resulting in a 'deterioration and disappearance of the species'.

In fact there was a double bind operating in Victorian England; education and work would damage the reproductive function, while that same reproductive function made women unfit for responsibility, power or equality. As the board of a university claimed in 1877:

> Education is greatly to be desired but it is better that the future matrons of the state should be without a university training than that it be produced at the fearful expense of ruined health; better that the future mothers of the state should be robust, hearty, healthy women, than that by over study they entail upon their descendants the germs of disease.
>
> (Smith-Rosenberg and Rosenberg 1973: 341–2)

Yet simultaneously, it was being argued that women's mental powers were not equal to those of men, and thus education would presumably be wasted. As Darwin stated in 1896:

> The chief distinction in the intellectual powers of the two sexes is shown by man's attaining to a higher eminence, in whatever he takes up, than can women. . . . If men are capable of a decided preeminence over women in many subjects, the average mental power in man must be above that of women.
>
> (Sayers 1982: 94)

Thus women's bodies either were damaged by education or work, or acted to make women unfit for this same work.

In nineteenth-century Britain it was almost universally accepted that the brain was directly linked to the reproductive organs (Showalter 1987) and therefore any interference in either the brain or the reproductive organs would affect the whole system. The brain and the uterus were conceptualized as being in competition for vital resources and energy, so that to concentrate one's resources in one was to deprive the other.

> The doctors and psychologists . . . conceded that it was possible for a woman, if she were sufficiently determined, to dodge the destiny prepared for her by untold eons of evolutionary struggle, and throw in her lot with the brain. But the resulting 'mental woman', if we may so term this counterpart to the natural 'uterine woman', could only hope to be a freak, morally and medically.
>
> (Ehrenreich and English 1979: 116)

Women were seen as 'victims of periodicity': likely to suffer from 'reflex insanity' as a result of their 'feminine functions'. Women's absence in the workforce or in education was described as evidence of their intellectual inferiority, resulting from woman's 'reproductive specialization'. None of the scholars of the day, who insisted on the necessity of keeping women in the home to protect them from the evils of the world, saw any connection between their absence from education and the workforce and the limited opportunities open to them. The absence of women proved their inability to compete with men, rather than men's failure to grant them the opportunity. Unfortunately this attitude is still pervasive today, as this comment in an American magazine shows:

> The fact that women have not made large inroads into fields such as engineering, in which a high degree of spatial ability is needed, is clearly due to something more fundamental than the hostility of male engineers. It is due, in part at least, to biology.
>
> (Lamott 1977: 43)

Nineteenth-century madness

Towards the end of the nineteenth century women were beginning to question and challenge openly the narrow role prescribed for them. Within the male-dominated Victorian society this was a crisis: not only was the future of the species in question should women reject their natural destiny, but individual women were likely to suffer from madness, insanity and destruction. All women's madness, illness and deviant behaviour was traditionally located in the womb; malfunctions or diseases of the reproductive organs were seen as being at the root of women's 'deviances'. Conversely, the reproductive capability was seen as being detrimentally affected by women's deviant behaviour. Early medical interventions for a wide range of illnesses experienced by women were centred on the womb, the matrix of all problems. As a Dr Direx wrote in 1869:

> Women are treated for diseases of the stomach, liver, kidneys, heart, lungs etc.; yet in most instances, these diseases will be found on due investigation, to be, in reality, no diseases at all,

but merely the sympathetic reactions or the symptoms of one disease, namely, a disease of the womb.

(Direx 1869: 23–4)

The institution of 'hysteria' as an explanation for most 'deviant' female behaviour in the nineteenth century is representative of this whole body of opinion which located the centre of women's existence in their reproductive capacities. 'Hysteria' became the umbrella term for those female 'problems' generally attributed to the propensity of modern nineteenth-century women to defy their 'nature', to question their role as childbearers and to assume the rights of men. Of course these 'hysterical' women were not actually suffering from a biological or pathological illness: they were, in the main, suffering from the oppression of a society which demanded almost total subservience and passivity. Many of the women diagnosed as hysterical were more independent and assertive than other women in their peer group. In 1867, Skey observed that hysterical women exhibit: 'more than the usual force and decision of character, of strong resolution, fearless of danger, bold riders, having plenty of what is termed nerve' (Skey 1867: 78). These strong-willed women were rejecting the traditional feminine role, refusing to be passive and inactive, and were thus posing a threat to the very foundations of Victorian society. The almost universal acceptance of 'hysteria' thus became the use of a diagnosis of illness to neutralize those who posed a threat to the dominant social order, invalidating and depoliticizing the challenge which these women presented by locating their problems within individual pathology. Hysteria as a syndrome contained a vast array of symptoms, from fainting, choking, sobbing, laughing, and paralysis, to general unhappiness, nervousness, or discontent. 'Hysterical' became synonymous with 'feminine': the essence of hysteria was seen to be part of the essence of femininity. Emotionality, lability and irrationality all combined to produce the hysterical personality, who was seen as being as inherently unreliable as she was inherently feminine.

At particular phases in her life cycle, a woman was seen as being particularly vulnerable to hysteria. Puberty, pregnancy, and the menopause were the phases of the life cycle most plagued with instability and suffering.

Women become insane during pregnancy, after parturition,

during lactation; at the age when the catemania (menstruation) first appear and when they disappear . . . the sympathetic connection between the brain and the uterus is plainly seen by the most casual observer.

(Blandford 1871: 71)

Nor was hysteria the only nervous disease which afflicted women, and which could explain a myriad of behaviours. Neurasthenia, a disease first diagnosed in North America, was a second nervous disorder which afflicted nineteenth-century women. It was a collection of varying symptoms, many of them similar to those of hysteria, including headaches, masturbation, vertigo, insomnia, and depression. Neurasthenia generally affected single women, 'in some way not in a condition for performing [their] reproductive function'. Women who had ambitions and desires, conscious and unconscious, which could not be realized in rigid Victorian society, became victims of the collection of symptoms labelled neurasthenia.

The doctors of the nineteenth century disagreed over the aetiology of hysterical and nervous illnesses in women: many believed that their patients were 'petty tyrants', attempting to exert their own will upon their families; others labelled the women as malingerers, attempting to avoid their womanly duties. The combination of invalidism and violent fits of rage exhibited by many of these women proved perplexing for the medical men, who generally chose to blame women's biological weakness for their problems. Anatomy as destiny, the womb as the centre of women's being, became the accepted ideology of the medical profession, providing the basis for their diagnosis. However, if one looks at the women who were diagnosed as suffering from these nervous disorders and the restrictive lives they were forced to live, the interpretation of historian Carroll Smith-Rosenberg (1972) seems more accurate: she proposed that these women, in having an hysterical fit, were using the only acceptable means of expressing rage, anger, or energy open to them. As nineteenth-century women became increasingly vocal about their discontent their doctors began to see the diseases of hysteria and neurasthenia everywhere. They applied this diagnosis to every woman who spoke of women's rights or who attempted an independent act. Thus women who rebelled could be defined as sick and confined to the home, to a life of passivity:

With hysteria, the cult of female invalidism was carried to its logical conclusion. Society had assigned affluent women to a life of confinement and inactivity, and medicine had justified this assignment by describing women as innately sick. In the epidemic of hysteria, women were both accepting their inherent 'sickness' and finding a way to rebel against an intolerable social role. Sickness, having become a way of life, became a way of rebellion, and medical treatment, which had always had strong overtones of coercion, revealed itself as frankly and brutally repressive.

(Ehrenreich and English 1979: 125)

The women who were labelled as hysterics were largely educated and unmarried, or seeking to challenge their allotted role, having ambitions for some independence or a career. When their ambitions were thwarted, these women experienced distress, anger, and illness as a result, expressing their emotions in the only ways which were available to them. As their doctors did not care to address the socio-political conditions underlying their deviant behaviour, the internal pathological model best fitted the bill. In addition to disorders of the womb, the repression or concealment of unnatural sexual feelings was perceived to be at the root of some nervous illnesses, with symptoms often manifested in masturbation, which thus led to the contention that clitoridectomy was an appropriate 'cure' for women's problems, as we shall see below.

The neurologist Horatio Donkin was one of the few progressive thinkers of the nineteenth century who acknowledged that nervous afflictions could be caused by the conflict between women's desire for independence and fulfilment and oppressive social restrictions. Donkin was personally acquainted with a number of forward-thinking women, whose 'nervous illnesses' were a direct result of their inability to combine the ideals of an independent womanhood with their role as a 'good' Victorian woman. However, despite his apparent insight, he finally concluded that hysteria was the result of 'unsatisfied sexual and maternal drives' (Showalter 1987), rather than cultural oppression, showing that even someone who could see the oppression of women resorted to the biological explanation.

Thus Victorian doctors conceptualized and 'treated' hysterical or deviant women within their medical model. They attributed distress to internal biological factors usually associated with the womb, and then treated women accordingly. These 'treatments' could be brutal in the extreme:

> a course of injections into the rectum, introduction of ice and water into the vagina and leeching of the labia. The suddenness with which the leeches applied to this part will fill themselves considerably increases the good effects of their application, and for some hours after their removal there is an oozing of blood from the leech bites.
>
> (Smith 1848: 601)

The historian Ann Douglas Wood (1973) documented the comments of a famous gynaecologist, Dr Bennet, who advocated 'placing the leeches right on the vulva, or the neck of the uterus, (and) cautioned the doctor to count them as they fell off, lest he lose some'. Bennet had known adventurous leeches to advance into the cervical cavity of the uterus itself, and he noted, 'I think I have scarcely ever seen more acute pain than experienced by several of my patients under these circumstances'.

The random application of such treatments makes chilling reading. For example, the specific 'insanity' to which Smith (above) applied his skills was manifested in a wide range of symptoms, such as 'eating like a ploughman', masturbation, attempted suicide, erotic tendencies, cussedness, and dysmenorrhea. A contemporary treatment for this female insanity, advocated by Dr Baker Brown, was clitoridectomy: removal of the clitoris, and frequently the labia as well. This was seen as a means of treating a wide range of manifestations of hysterial female madness, ranging from women who were not interested in the courtship advances of men, or who were 'indifferent to the social influences of domestic life', to those who challenged the confinements of their narrow female role. Brown cited as successful cases women who had wished to take advantage of the new 1857 divorce act and who returned to their husbands following treatment by clitoridectomy. As Showalter (1987) comments: 'clitoridectomy is the surgical enforcement of an ideology which restricts female sexuality to reproduction' (Showalter 1987: 77).

Ovariectomy, or removal of the ovaries (often termed 'female castration'), was probably the most common 'cure' for female ailments. As Ehrenreich and English commented: 'In 1906 a leading gynaecological surgeon estimated that there were 150,000 women in the United States who had lost their ovaries under the knife (1979: 111). All these medical interventions were often combined with the confinement of the woman, away from the temptations of the world which were at the root of her illness. An analogy has been made between this seclusion treatment and a game of chess, a battle between the woman and her physician:

> The medical idea of a full and radical cure took the form of a kind of moral checkmate — the complete submission of the patient to the physician's authority, with a full confession of moral wretchedness and the various tricks and artifices involved in the presentation of the 'symptoms'.

(Clarke 1981: 295)

The standard 'rest cure' of the American neurologist Silas Mitchell consisted of seclusion, massage, immobility, electricity, and bland diet (Showalter 1987). It was a treatment which closely resembles the kinds of torture used on political prisoners in more modern times in order to break their resolves, disorientating them through sensory deprivation. The women were isolated from their family and friends, allowed no activities or communication (not even being allowed to sit up in bed) and fed numerous large meals by a nurse. This 'cure' resulted in women being more than willing to accept the dictates of their doctors in order to leave the rest room.

Thus women's 'reproductive specialization' was invoked to maintain their inferior position in Victorian society. If a woman seemed to be rejecting her reproductive role, in wanting to have a career, live independently of men or not marry, this could be attributed to imbalances in her reproductive system: her 'raging hormones'. As G. Windolz noted in an analysis of nineteenth-century psychiatry, all behaviour which was defined as deviant was labelled as illness: 'As members of the medical profession, psychiatrists considered deviant behaviour as mental illness. Like all illnesses, mental illness required medical care and attention' (Windolz 1987: 291).

As we have seen, the care and attention proffered was based on the misogynist dogma which masqueraded as medical knowledge. This was as true at the end of the Victorian era as it was at the beginning when there was little regulation of medical practice. (Before the Medical Qualifications Act of 1858 it was possible for any Master of Arts from Oxford or Cambridge University to become a medical doctor by giving three written, or six spoken, lectures, on the works of Galen.)

What relevance, it might be asked, does the appalling treatment which many women received at the hands of the Victorian medical profession have for women today? Many feminist historians have challenged the ideologies inherent in these practices, exposing the misogynist nature of the beliefs which associate woman's madness, badness, or unhappiness with her reproductive cycle and her sexuality. Unfortunately, many of these explanations for women's experiences of distress have been perpetuated in different forms and remain with us to this day. Hysteria and neurasthenia have been replaced by the modern 'diseases' of the premenstrual syndrome, postnatal depression and the menopausal deficiency syndrome. While clitoridectomy and seclusion in solitary confinement are no longer accepted 'treatments', chemotherapy, electroconvulsive therapy, and hysterectomy are just a few of the interventions which have taken their place. Women are as effectively numbed and silenced by these modern treatments as they were by the Victorian 'cures'.

The association between 'nervous disorder', as manifested in a wide range of symptoms, and the biological events of the female reproductive cycle is as prevalent now as it was in the nineteenth century, even though it may appear in a more subtle form today. Science has progressed rapidly in the last decade, allowing more sophisticated explanations of female madness to evolve: explanations which are no further towards an understanding of a woman's experience than those of the early psychiatrists who spoke of 'proxysms' of the brain being caused by menstruation.

The nineteenth-century biological arguments may seem outdated, but they are still used to define and confine women, as well as being used to exclude women from highly paid jobs in industry. Reproduction and menstruation are used as controlling factors in women's lives, as women are defined by their reproductive status, their position in the life cycle or life course: thus the idea that 'anatomy is destiny' is reinforced.

Twentieth-century madness

Betty Friedan, in her analysis of the 'feminine mystique' (1963), described how twentieth-century women are confined by their reproductive cycles as surely as were their sisters of 100 years before. Although advances in equal opportunities have made education and employment open to all women, Friedan observed that the women who were going through college in North America in the 1960s were in the majority rejecting any intellectual or professional career, concentrating instead on their future as a wife and mother. The education which had been hard won by the early feminists seemed to be being rejected: women were instead fulfilling their biological role, to the exclusion of all else. However, this was not because these women were not capable of success:

> The girls' evasion of growth in college is explained by the fact that for a girl, identity is exclusively sexual; for the girl, college itself is seen even by these scholars not as a key to a larger identity but as a disguised 'outlet for sexual impulses'.
>
> (Friedan 1963: 143)

The discontent experienced by women who assumed this 'predestined' role of wife and mother was attributed to the high level of education they had received. The obvious answer to this, in the eyes of some educators, was to exclude women from four-year college courses, courses which could be filled by men, so that women's expectations would coincide with their 'natural' role as wife and mother. Again, attempts to exclude women from education were legitimated by referring to the importance of the reproductive role. Just as the woman in 1860 was defined by her biology, so was the woman in 1960. The opportunities were greater in 1960, but the internalization of the idea that fulfilment for women is through childrearing and consumer spending was as powerful in restricting women as were the nineteenth-century treatises by male psychiatrists.

I would argue that society has not progressed much further in the 1980s. Women are still socialized into looking to their biology and their sexuality for identity and self-definition, even as we are tantalized with images of the independent career woman, who appears to have escaped her reproductive chains.

Reproduction: exaggerated or ignored

the natural mysteries of childbirth and menstruation are as directly convincing as death itself, and remain to this day what they must also have been in the beginning, primary sources of religious awe.

(Campbell 1972: 372)

Is it because of this sense of awe that there is so little discussion of the female body, of reproduction, in the writings of our culture, either in literature or science? Is this why it is not seen as a valid area of study, and is ignored in analyses of the human lifespan? I think not: it is part of the practice which ignores experiences which are peculiar to women when discussing 'people', at the same time as emphasizing the infirmity in women ascribed to these same ignored experiences.

The need to acknowledge the validity of the study of the female body and reproduction is an important issue. Now as in the last century it is used as a justification for gender inequalities, but is seldom considered in 'lifespan studies', studies of human development throughout the life cycle. As with other areas of psychology, the male has been taken to be the norm, so that neither reproduction nor cyclicity is seen as an important aspect of experience. Any psychological work which acknowledges the existence of cyclicity as an influence on women's behaviour tends to examine only the problems, the 'syndromes', thus reinforcing the negative stereotypes. Conversely, feminists have argued that we should deny the effects of biology, deny the effects of experiences such as menstruation, and recouch the experience in positive terms, arguing that negative experiences are merely the result of negative social constructions (Delaney *et al.* 1976: 24). Yet as Janet Sayers argues, it is not enough to look solely to social−constructionist explanations, to deny the influence of the female body, as reproduction does have real effects on women's lives:

The denial, on grounds of abstract principle, that menstruation has any negative aspects . . . does not . . . as is sometimes implied, necessarily serve the interests of women. . . . Certainly it is important to dispel unwarranted and superstitious social constructions and beliefs about women's biology. Much of the scientific and often feminist-inspired research into the actual, as opposed to the assumed, effects of menstruation on behaviour has been extremely useful in this way to the cause of women. If this cause is to be fully served, however, it is also essential to acknowledge that biology (menstruation, in this case), does have real effects on women's lives and that these effects are not to be dismissed as merely the result of the ideas that societies entertain about them.

(Sayers 1982: 123–4)

If this is not recognised, these important life stages for all women, of menarche, menstruation, pregnancy and the menopause, are either exaggerated or ignored.

Much of the psychological work on gender identity development (or lifespan research) ignores menstruation, pregnancy, and the menopause. This is a phenomenon which has many parallels in other areas of study where the experiences of women are denied any importance or credibility. However, it is a position which is not unchallenged within psychology. A new body of research is developing, pioneered by the work of Carol Gilligan (1977) and others, in which many of the traditional theories based solely on male samples have been deconstructed to show that they cannot be applied to female samples. For example, Gilligan has deconstructed Kohlberg's (1966) theory of moral development, applied it to a female sample and demonstrated that the constructs for development used by the original author do not take account of gender differences. It is equally important that in theories of development we recognise the importance of reproduction — of menstruation, pregnancy and the menopause — as real experiences for women which cannot be ignored. This is not to say that women are determined by these events in the life cycle, as nineteenth-century physicians all declared, but we cannot deny that they exist, and to ignore them is to ignore an important part of a woman's experience.

Cultural connections

I will argue that we need to examine both the social constructions of the female body, the 'cultual connections' that are made and the way in which biological changes are experienced by women. We need to look at both the wider social context in which the female body is understood and at the context of the individual woman and the influence which her own conceptualizations of her body have on her experience, status and identity. The female body and reproduction are largely constructed in a derogatory light with the potential for debilitation emphasized, resulting in many women having a negative self-image. These social constructions often contribute towards the experience of negative symptoms associated with reproduction. For although menstruation or pregnancy may have strong biological components, there is no biological basis for the myths and misconceptions which act to define women as inferior or second rate, because of their 'bleeding wombs', or as inevitably ill as a result in the reproduction cycle.

When I talk of this reproductive cycle I am referring to the whole cycle from menarche to menopause, not merely the menstrual cycle which occurs every month. It is within this whole reproductive cycle that I will examine the psychology of the female body. For puberty will be seen to mark the beginning of the process which links female reproduction to weakness and debilitation, defining women through our position in the reproductive life cycle. For it is following menarche that the 'girl' becomes a woman, and following menopause that society deems women useless and redundant. I will follow this process through the entire cycle in order to show how the same processes operate at each stage. Women's sexuality is categorized in our society as being intrinsically related to reproduction. The premenarcheal or postmenopausal female is viewed as asexual, which serves to cloak female sexuality divorced from reproduction in a mantle of secrecy and shame. Yet at the same time as defining a woman as sexual if she has the capacity to reproduce, the sexual element in menstruation, pregnancy, and the menopause is denied or ignored, creating further consternation and confusion.

Women split: good/bad, madonna/whore

A woman must continually watch herself. . . . From earliest childhood she must have been taught to survey herself continually. And so she comes to consider the surveyed and the surveyor within her as the two constituent yet always distinct elements of her identity as a woman.

(Berger 1972: 46−7)

13

John Berger recognizes the subject/object contradictions which face women, and which are inherently present in any analysis of the female body. Women cannot escape from the dichotomy of being surveyed, of being labelled and categorized, yet of simultaneously surveying ourselves, of placing ourselves in the scheme of things. One of the ways in which this contradiction operates is in the categorization of women within the madonna/whore framework, which describes the pure, virginal, 'good' woman on her pedestal, unspoiled by sex or sin: her counterpart, the whore, is consumed by desires of the flesh, is dangerous and inherently bad, tempting man from higher pursuits. The individual woman cannot be good *and* bad so she must be placed in one or other of the categories. This inevitably leads to consternation and splitting in the individual woman, who must deny one aspect of her experience. This splitting is something I will refer to throughout the book, examining how it affects women at different stages in the reproductive cycle. These archetypes are used to define and confine women, since behaviours which deviate from the reproductive norm are labelled bad or deviant.

Betty Friedan described a second archetype which she felt was becoming more powerful as a means of categorizing women than the old madonna/whore dichotomy: that of the feminine woman vs career woman:

> The new image opens a different fissure — the feminine woman, whose goodness includes the desires of the flesh, and the career woman, whose evil includes every desire of the separate self. The new feminine morality story is the exorcising of the forbidden career dream, the heroine's victory over Mephistopheles: the devil, first in the form of a career woman, who threatens to take away the heroine's husband or child, and finally, the devil inside the heroine herself, the dream of independence, the discontent of spirit, and even the feeling of a separate identity that must be exorcised in order to win.
>
> (Friedan 1963: 40)

If this particular archetype is more influential in defining women today, the female body is inherently part of it. The myths surrounding the female body are used as justifications for preventing women from pursuing careers, or for labelling career women as dangerous and bad: they are not seen as real women. It is not surprising then that the image of the independent woman as temptress is used to warn heterosexual men about the dangers of the AIDS virus in recent government television advertisements:

> The swish of nylons as long legs cross. Close ups of wet, licked lips, of painted eyes narrowing hawkishly. Fast cutting concentrates on elegant hands smoothing expensive (black) dress material over a pert, inviting bottom and on breasts that practically leer at the poor boy about to be shamelessly seduced. . . . The government's latest bash at alerting the heterosexual population to the HIV virus re-introduces Eve, the erotic vamp who lures men to their doom. All those guilty impulses. . . . Just as femme [sic] fatales emerged as scary icons after WW2 to warn threatened males about the dark flipside of Rosie the Riveter, today's post-pill, post-feminist, condom age update makes female independence — indeed female choice — frightening.
>
> (Lyttle 1988: 21)

Individual women are inevitably positioned at either end of the dichotomy: good/bad, madonna/whore, feminine/career-orientated, and their position is often determined by their reproductive status. For example, the woman who is a mother cannot be a good mother and a sexual person at the same time, both madonna and whore; women's sexuality is dangerous and threatening and is therefore at odds with the stereotype of the 'good mother'. This welter of images forms a large part of the contradictory discourses which both define and prescribe behaviour. In the discourse of 'woman' in our society, reproduction is used both to explain and dismiss behaviour and experiences. Women's bodies, menstruation, pregnancy and the menopause contribute to the stereotypes of women — stereotypes which are used as a standard by which to judge women as good or bad, sane or mad.

> Two ideas flow side by side: one, that the female body is impure, corrupt, the site of discharges, bleedings, dangerous to masculinity, a source of moral and physical contamination, 'the devil's gateway'. On the other hand, as mother, the woman is beneficent, sacred, pure, asexual, nourishing; and the physical potential for motherhood — that same body with its bleedings and mysteries — is her single destiny and justification in life.
>
> (Rich 1986: 34)

This analysis of the psychology of the female body and the discourses of reproduction is not without problems. As Sue Condor has shown, by drawing attention to the way in which women are oppressed and subordinated by these discourses 'we may present an objectified, pathologized image of women as passive victims of social forces' (Condor 1986). Although the analysis of this book is intended to refute myths and produce a new feminist psychology of the female body, I am aware of the inherent danger of reinforcing negative images of women as they are at present. Condor quotes Zavalloni in discussing this, who comments that 'Even if it is seen as the result of oppression, the imputation that (low status group members) possess a damaged identity is an additional derogatory social representation thrown into the field of social interaction' (Zavalloni 1973: 68). Thus by drawing attention to the negative effects of the discourses of reproduction on women's identity I may be in danger of adding to them. However, before women can challenge these belief systems and construct analyses of experience which are not misogynist, it is necessary for us to identify the negative effects of the present system of knowledge. The benefits in this, which enable us to work towards a reconceptualization of women's experience, will outweigh the potential damaging effects as long as this analysis becomes a further step towards the creation of a new system of knowledge. For it will be possible to examine the positive aspects of reproduction which will form the very basis for our reconstructed system of knowledge, as well as providing a greater understanding of the roots of distress associated with the reproductive cycle. It is time that the silence within psychology surrounding women's reproductive life cycle is broken — regardless of the possibility of some reinforcement of the stereotypes — as silence can only achieve just that, whilst discussion can provide alternative explanations. Discussion can challenge the images of women contained within the present discourse and open the arena for a new understanding of the psychology of the female body, whilst silence can only maintain oppression.

What is essential is that we have an understanding of the truths surrounding cyclicity on female identity, including the effects of menstruation on behaviour and the effects of major life events such as pregnancy and the menopause. These uniquely female experiences should not be ignored or denied, nor should their influence be exaggerated. The silence which surrounds the reality of the female experience needs to be broken.

Finally: removing the frame

It is possible to deconstruct the negative images of the female body, and the stereotypes of women associated with the reproductive cycle, through a careful examination of how the discourses surrounding menarche, menstruation, pregnancy and the menopause are used in 'framing' women's experiences.

Framing involves placing boundaries around women: boundaries around our behaviour which are limiting and act to prevent growth or change. Framing defines behaviour and experiences: providing explanations for those experiences which fit within the framework, whilst at the same time defining as deviant those behaviours which do not. But women's reproductive capacity need not imprison us. By offering alternative explanations and definitions of behaviour and experiences we can break out of the frame. Reclaiming our bodies from the restrictive framework, and finding a more flexible repertoire of options for expression, is long overdue.

Chapter 2

The invisible woman

> puberty, which gives man the knowledge of greater power, gives to woman the knowledge of her dependence.
>
> (Tilt 1852: 265)

The discourses which define and confine women (through identifying their purportedly scientific version of women's sexuality and reproductive capacities, their 'nature', as the essence of their whole identity) first come into being with the girl approaching puberty. A period of the life cycle seen as a time of 'miniature insanity' in the Victorian era (Tilt 1852), puberty is a transitional period, marking the entrance of the young girl into her new role as a woman. It is during adolescence and puberty that the discourse which locates the centre of a woman's being in her womb, in her sexuality, is first found, and the seeds of contempt and disgust towards a woman's body and her reproductive function first sown.

The definition of women as weak, inferior and inherently unstable because of their dangerous sexuality and 'bleeding wombs' has long been the basis of society's and psychology's understanding of female adolescence, concealing reality behind the myth. It is during adolescence that the young woman first experiences a split between her body and her self: between her own experience and the archetype she is expected to emulate.

In most societies, men and women develop very different attitudes towards their bodies and their sexuality; in general the positive, almost proud attitude of men contrasts sharply with the negative, and often guilt-ridden feelings of many women.

Sexuality concealed

The way in which the visible sexual organs, the genitals, are construed by society, and these constructions internalized by males and females, is representative of the stereotype 'male = good, female = bad' sex difference. From infancy, boys develop a greater understanding of their sexual organs, which are more visible and easily named than those of girls. Shopper (1979) reported how mothers are more reluctant to name the genital organs of their daughters than of their sons, and tend to do it at a much later age. Health professionals as well as lay people confound this problem by mislabelling the visible vulva the vagina, undoubtedly a result of a combination of embarrassment and ignorance surrounding female genitalia. Thus adolescent girls approach puberty with an inaccurate understanding of their own sexual organs, most having no conceptualization of the clitoris at all (Rosenbaum 1979). It has also been claimed that many girls conceptualize their genitals as having only one excretory opening which is devoid of any sexuality (Shopper 1979), and as having solely a cloacal function, associated with excretion, dirt and badness. Thus whilst boys learn to perceive their genitals as a source of pride and pleasure, girls mainly develop a sense of shame, disgust and humiliation about theirs. In this way, social stereotypes which define women's genitals as unpleasant, odorous and unattractive, are internalized by the female child.

Many feminists have emphasized the role which language plays in the construction, perpetuation, and representation of women's oppression. This debate is not one which I can discuss in detail in this book, but it is of importance in an analysis of the invisibility of the female genitalia. One relevant argument is that language is 'man-made', and either denies the existence of sexuality in women or provides words which have negative connotations.

Only male sexual characteristics have been named as 'real' within the patriarchal framework, so despite any contrary evidence which female anatomy may reveal, there is doubt about the existence of female 'sex'. So powerful is language in structuring thought and reality that it can 'blind' its users to the evidence of the physical world; objects and entities remain but shadowy entities when they are not named.

(Spender 1980: 172)

The absence of positive and appropriate language to describe a woman's sexual organs contrasts sharply with the number of words which can be used to describe the male sexual organs. Anne Dickson (1986) described the female genitals as either 'eclipsed' or 'exposed' by the language used in our culture. Descriptive terms such as: 'down there, privates, crotch, it, she/her, rude bits, sex, waterworks, between your legs, bottom . . .', strengthen the view that a woman's genitals are something mysterious, vague and taboo: 'eclipsed' through the avoidance of naming. The other extreme is 'exposure', where the enigma and mystery are replaced by more explicit, derogatory terms: 'pussy, beaver, muff, bush, man-trap, crack, cunt, hole, slit, gash, twat, etc.'.

Illustrations and photographs, either in the form of 'artistic' drawings or blatant pornography, can also be seen to reflect this eclipsed–exposed dichotomy. The classical portrayal of the eclipsed female genitals in art form is as a slit, the symbolic 'dash or stroke', which contrasts with the usually graphic and detailed depiction of the male genitals. The depiction of women in pornography is indisputably 'exposed', as women are portrayed as objects, reduced to graphically photographed 'parts'.

> the staple of porn will always be the naked female body . . . genitals exposed, because as man devised it, her naked body is the female's 'shame', her private parts the private property of man, whilst his are the ancient, holy, universal, patriarchal instrument of his power, his rule by force over her.
>
> (Brownmiller 1975: 32)

The eclipsing of the genitals is also perpetuated by the influential literature of the medical profession:

> mentally convinced that women were without sex, the medical profession dutifully reproduced diagrams which reflected fantasies and not the facts. And in the process of propagating their mythologies, the medical profession created a difficult situation for many females who were required to reconcile the fantasy with the facts. Once more women were required to accommodate their physiology to a male version of reality.
>
> (Spender 1980: 173)

This criticism is mainly levelled at more traditional medical texts, which have avoided accurate representation in preference of the symbolic single line as a depiction of the female genitals. The effect of this on women, who in general have no access to accurate representations of female genitals, is tremendous, as they can learn to hate, fear, and despise what they perceive to be a taboo part of the body. Although the black and white anatomical pencil drawings which are to be found in more recent texts (as well as in many women's self-help books) provide more information, they are still far removed from reality, as the dissected, splayed labia bears little resemblance to most women's knowledge of their own genitals.

A new generation of feminist artists, such as Judy Chicago, Betty Dodson, Georgia O'Keefe, and Shelly Lowell, are challenging the traditional images of women's bodies and particularly their genitals through their art. There is some controversy associated with the 'vaginal iconology' — in which the female genitals are redefined and celebrated in both a positive and explicit way — as it is seen as reinforcing womb-centred, biologically deterministic ways of thinking. Yet this celebration of the female genitals, through drawings, photographs, plaster casts, and many other media, is an unequivocal challenge to the absence of the female genitals in masculine culture (Tickner 1987).

There is also a move to encourage young girls as well as older women to explore their own genitals, or those of other women, using a speculum and a mirror (Dickson 1986). This allows women to gain intimate knowledge of their own vulva, vagina, and cervix, and could have the additional benefit of early detection of cervical abnormalities. (Many women greet the suggestion of self-examination with horror, which only serves to illustrate the strength of the taboo surrounding female sexuality and the female genitals.)

Yet obtaining a speculum is not a straightforward matter. In an article in the *Guardian* in July 1987, Suzie Hayman reported that Boots, the largest retail chemist in Britain, had informed her that speculums were not available for sale to the public, for 'medical reasons'. Apparently it was felt that women should only examine their own cervix under the supervision of a qualified doctor. This reinforces the belief that a woman's body is not her own territory but that of the medical profession, a belief which forms part of the discourse of reproductive captivity throughout the life cycle, as we shall see. The medical profession may argue that women might examine themselves with unsterilized instruments and thereby introduce infection. However, this is an illogical concern: 'the speculum used in the home may well not be a sterile instrument, but then neither on the whole is the penis' (Roberts 1981: 9).

A woman's sexuality, her genital organs, and their implicit function, are either denied or exploited. This dichotomy has the effect of creating confusion and conflict for the adolescent, who in general has little awareness of her own sexuality and her developing sexual organs. If she is not ignorant of her genital structure the young girl may internalize the belief represented by Freud's comment that: 'the woman's genital structure is deficient — a wound which is the result of a previous and unremembered castration' (Penfold and Walker 1984: 74).

Focusing on the breasts

It has been suggested (Rosenbaum 1979) that the relative lack of visibility of the female genitals, both literally and within the discourse concerning women's sexuality, results in breast development occupying great importance in the adolescent consciousness. However, there is a notable lack of information available on the normal process of breast development, a surprising fact considering the influence of breasts on a woman's identity and self-image. The breasts are important outward signs of sexuality for the developing woman, and remain so during adult life. The mass media in Britain and the US, obsessed with photographs of women's breasts, reinforce this important role for the breasts in female sexual identity. Women are objectified and dehumanized, represented as sexual: their sole function being to serve man's pleasure. The discourse of a woman's body as unclean, soiled, her sexuality split from her reproductive self, is perpetuated by this objectification: 'The little boy who draws two dark, angry circles on the poster of a fully clothed woman has already absorbed society's lesson: the nipples on his chest are invulnerable and sexless but a girl's are shameful and dirty' (Brownmiller 1984: 45).

The paradox that women's breasts glare out from almost every tabloid newspaper and are used to sell all manner of consumer durables, yet a woman who bares her own breasts in public could be arrested for indecent exposure, points to the anomaly that men have more access to and control over women's bodies than women themselves. It is ironic that breastfeeding an infant in public is still widely frowned upon, denying the natural function of the breasts at the same time as objectifying them for the sexual gratification of men. As Susan Brownmiller has noted:

> How ironic that the sight of a mother breastfeeding her baby is so unnerving to many of the people who like to see — or to show — some cleavage in a dinner dress. In a curious reversal the suckling infant actually becomes the embarrassing stand-in for the adult male lover. The nipple tease is the historic basis for decolletage in fashion: a certain amount of exposure is sexy but an accidental display of the areola is crudely beyond the pale.
>
> (Brownmiller 1984: 45)

The archetypal dichotomy of the madonna/whore is reinforced within this discourse, as only the whore would bare her breasts (despite the traditional depiction of the Madonna suckling the infant Jesus).

The promotion of these images of 'perfect' breasts makes the average woman feel imperfect, and makes her conceptualize her visible breasts — rather than her less visible vulva — as her main erogenous zone. This can result in the need for psycho-sexual counselling for women who have undergone breast surgery, and as a result of it see their sexual life as having ended. For the developing adolescent this can result in worry about normality of breast development; anxiety if one breast appears to be growing faster than the other; or insecurity if one's peers appear to be at a higher stage of development. Yet these experiences will be common for many young women, as physical growth is rarely uniform within any cohort of adolescents. Young women fear that their breasts are too large or too small; not the 'right' shape; the nipples not the 'right' size. Satisfaction is rare:

> Slight and slender were my grown-up ambitions. Too often for comfort my mother, statuesque and on the heavy side, had teased (in front of my father) that I was going to inherit her ample bosom. No I won't, I'd mutter, in awe of what I'd seen when we'd share a bath. Even worse was the fear that I might not develop at all, that I'd be wearing undershirts for the rest of my life.
>
> (Brownmiller 1984: 25)

The purchase of the first bra is still an important stage in the developing identity of many girls as it symbolizes an outward change, yet many mothers encourage their daughters to acquire this particular yoke of womanhood when they have scarcely begun to develop breasts. Conversely, other mothers will refuse to acknowledge that any change is taking place. Either attitude on the part of the mother may have serious effects on the development of her daughter's self-image, whilst conflicts between the desires of the young woman and her mother over this issue may further isolate the adolescent girl at this difficult stage of life.

I remember when my mother finally relented in the face of my persistent complaints about being the odd one out, and bought me an A-cup which I couldn't quite fill. I immediately locked myself away and tried on everything I could lay my hands on, inspecting my new profile in the mirror. My pride in those two bumps was rooted in the tender conviction that reaching adult womanhood would confer on me all the significance and love I would need.

(Dickson 1986: 33)

Yet despite the importance of breast development to the emerging adolescent identity, it is menarche, the first menstrual period, which provides a focus for the continuous physical and psychological changes which are occurring throughout puberty.

Menarche: the arrival of Eve's curse or a celebration of womanhood?

Menarche tends to occur relatively late in puberty, following the beginning of the physical changes: the development of pubic hair, breast development and the gradual widening of the hips. There is evidence that only about 25 per cent of girls are prepared for menarche adequately (Bloch 1972). As a result, many myths and negative assumptions surrounding menstruation are frequently internalized. When education does take place it is usually in a way which divorces menstruation from reality, from sexuality, and from the change in status from child to woman. Menstrual education is concerned primarily with hygiene and biology, in a way which is disconnected from girls' experience. Biological explanations, which are remote from her experience and are based on abstract concepts, will have little meaning or significance for the adolescent and will therefore be of little use. Teaching methods emphasize anatomy, physiology, and hormones, and avoid any discussion of the reality of menstruation or the pertinent practical issues. My own school, for example, used the model of the reproductive system of the rabbit in order to discuss reproductive function, which is hardly of direct relevance to the pubescent girl coming to terms with her own changing body and developing sexuality. As P. McKeever notes: 'This treatment of menarche as simply a biological event reflects the strong cultural avoidance of menstruation' (McKeever 1984: 423).

Many women recall menarche as the focal point for all of the different physical developments and psychological adjustments which take place during puberty. Menarche allows accommodation and assimilation of these changes to take place, as it is an event which cannot be ignored and for many mothers and daughters symbolizes the beginning of womanhood, a *rite de passage*. Girls themselves have reported that menarche confirms their identity as a woman, their ability to reproduce, and has a profound effect on their relationships with their parents (Danza 1983; McKeever 1984).

In Victorian England, when problems of hygiene were greater and the boundaries placed on women's lives more severe, menarche signalled the imposition of restrictions and confinements that would continue throughout adult life. 'Physical activities, travelling, exercise and study were curtailed and forbidden . . . and social life outside the home [was] restricted to a few safe contacts with other girls, clergymen or local philanthropists' (Showalter 1987: 57).

In society today, out-of-role or tomboy behaviour is less acceptable postmenarche (Sharpe 1981) when the adolescent girl is encouraged to conform to the female role model. This loss of freedom can feel like a punishment for being a woman, suddenly having to refrain from previously acceptable pastimes, with no alternative and positive role being offered.

In her tree climbing days the ascent would have taken only a few minutes. But she had given up climbing when she started to grow her hair and stopped wearing shorts every day during the summer holidays. Since she was thirteen, when her periods began, she felt she was pregnant with herself, bearing the slowly ripening embryo of Melanie-grown-up inside herself for a gestation time the length of which she was not precisely aware. And, during this time, to climb a tree might provoke a miscarriage and she would remain forever stranded in childhood, a crop-haired tomboy.

(Carter 1986: 20)

In much of the discourse which shapes our understanding of adolescence, menarche is construed as being important because of its relationship to reproduction. It means that the young girl is now physically capable of becoming pregnant. It has been shown that womanhood and motherhood are often linked together in educational materials about menstruation (Whisnant and Zegans 1975), yet sexuality or identity changes are rarely discussed. However, this link with pregnancy is mostly erroneous, as adolescent girls are usually not fertile for the first few years following menarche, the first menstrual cycles being anovulatory. The inability of the educators to link sexuality and motherhood, or sexuality and menstruation, even at this early stage, acts to reinforce the split between a woman's body and her experience.

The idea that menarche implies the beginning of sexuality in a young girl is taboo, and may precipitate a family crisis as deeply-rooted conflicts surrounding childhood sexuality may be revealed. There is no attempt in contemporary Western society to prepare girls for the complexities of being physically able to bear children (and therefore openly sexual) yet with no legitimate outlet for their sexuality. The madonna/whore archetypes serve to instil the belief that girls who engage in any sexual activity are easy: 'slags' or 'sluts', and to limit women's behaviour further. Thus splits between body and self will be maintained, as the adolescent girl cannot reconcile her desire for an exploration of sexual activity with the stereotypes available. Sue Lees (1983) reinforced the impression that the double standards of sexuality for men and women were alive and well amongst a group of adolescent teenagers in her own recent study: as slags and sluts were clearly differentiated in the teenage population, often on a seemingly arbitrary basis, regardless of the actual activities of the girls themselves. If a boy was annoyed with a girl, a convenient means of revenge was to label her a slag, and thus damage her standing in the social group. This labelling has been shown to apply to all girls and has negative connotations whether or not the girls are labelled 'easy':

The boys had, of course, classified the girls into the familiar two categories: the slags who'd go with anyone and everyone (they were alright for a quick screw, but you'd never get serious about it) and the drags who didn't but whom you might one day think about going steady with.

(Robins and Cohen 1978: 58)

Whilst it was acceptable, even praiseworthy, for the boys to brag about their sexual conquests, nice girls, or drags, remain pure and untouched, or barter their sexuality in exchange for security in a steady relationship. As Cowie and Lees note:

The construction of female sexuality seems to involve the construction of a difference between slags and drags: a certain kind of sexuality — essentially promiscuous/dirty in nature — is not natural for all girls/women but only resides in the slag. Yet non-slags are always viewed as possibly available, potential slags, until found to be drags or potential wives.

(Cowie and Lees 1987: 111)

These double standards are present in much of the discourse which moulds and maintains women's perceptions of their sexuality throughout adult life.

Parents who have internalized the double standards themselves and are overcome by fears of pregnancy in their adolescent daughters concentrate their attentions on the negative consequences of emerging sexuality, such as early pregnancy or loss of reputation. This instils fear in many girls and adds to the belief that women's sexuality is dangerous and must be surreptitious or denied. Two women whom I interviewed recalled their adolescent fears: 'After my first period I stopped playing rough games with the boys in my class. I had heard that you could get pregnant if one of them fell on top of you' (M.J.).

I seemed to spend the whole of my teenage years fending off the advances of the boys I went out with. It was an elaborate game involving giving enough to maintain their interest, yet not enough to mean that I would be called 'easy'. I remember feeling guilty and quite unclean the day I first went 'all the way': it felt as if I had let myself down. My boyfriend was over the moon.

(J.B.)

It is partly the strong taboo surrounding childhood sexuality which reinforces the divide between menstruation and sexual identity. For if parents and teachers are to acknowledge that the changes occurring at menarche cannot be separated from sexuality, they have to question many of their own assumptions and beliefs. Furthermore, the emphasis on the association between womanhood and motherhood is remote from the immediate life experiences of the girl, who is coming to terms with her own developing identity. The ideology which implies that womanhood is synonymous with motherhood reinforces the belief that the womb is the focal point of a woman's body, and the reproductive system the centre of her emotional life: the discourse of woman ruled by her womb. This connection, which is often internalized at this early stage, provides the backdrop for many anxieties and conflicts in later life, when women who have chosen an alternative career are made to regret that they have not borne children. If women are to have real choices, to be able to choose whether or not to be mothers, they must be made aware that being a woman does not necessitate being a mother.

This association of woman and mother also reinforces the notion that women are defined by their relationships: in this context, through either their relationships with men or with their children. Throughout the life cycle women are encouraged to seek self-definition, meaning and a role in life through their relationships with others — through friendships, love affairs, marriage and their children. This is not the case for men, as Gilligan noted:

> For women, the whole of identity is defined in the context of a relationship, and judged by a standard of responsibility and care. Although the world of the self that men describe at times includes people and 'deep attachments', no particular person or relationship is mentioned, nor is the activity of the relationship portrayed in the context of self description . . . the male 'I' is defined in separation.
>
> (Gilligan 1982: 160–1)

This discourse, which defines women through their relationships rather than as individuals, leads to crises when the relationships are not as fulfilling as the popular myths suggest (see below).

The emphasis on pregnancy, or avoidance of it, by the parents and teachers of the adolescent girl, also results in sexuality being defined in terms of heterosexual contact, penetration and impregnation. If adolescent girls believe that any sexuality if expressed can result in unwanted pregnancy or loss of reputation, it will be difficult for them to develop a positive sexual identity. This may result in many girls feeling that they can only cope with the changes which are taking place during puberty if they separate them entirely from themselves — thus perpetuating the split in identity.

Menarche is clearly an important event in the development of a woman's identity, yet in theories of identity development it is usually ignored. The traditional identity theorists such as Erikson concentrate on identity development in men, which precludes any discussion of phenomena experienced only by women, such as menstruation. Feminist critics such as Carol Gilligan have reconceptualized female identity development, stressing that constructs such as caring and affiliation are important categories to consider in the examination of female development, as well as the constructs of achievement, independence, etc. which it seems are of primary importance in identity development in men. Within an analysis which recognizes that there are gender differences in identity development, we need to acknowledge the importance of menarche, which symbolizes entry into womanhood.

At one level, of course, there is a strong biological component, with the first appearance of menstrual blood, largely determined by nutrition and growth, but menarche is also bound by discourse. For many girls, this is their first contact with the taboos and restrictions surrounding their bodies, their first contact with the discourses surrounding reproduction. At menarche the young woman is confronted with the conflicting societal messages which say she is now a woman. This should be a positive experience, a significant life event, yet great feelings of shame and secrecy surround it. The resulting confusion and disturbance is shown by the fact that many girls report that they felt they should be pleased, yet could not express their feelings (Whisnant and Zegans 1975). Girls are led to believe that some monumental change in status will occur, that menarche will transform their lives, and they feel let down.

One by one my classmates 'started' and you could see from the tell tale bulge in their navy blue knickers that womanhood was upon them. My day came on September 15, 1957. I was tremendously happy and excited, having no inherited theory about the pain and nuisance of menstruation. But when I told my mother she curiously confined me to bed and brought me breakfast on a tray. I wanted to tell my father and she said I mustn't. Inchoately I thought, if being a woman is a good thing, then why isn't there a public celebration of this biological event that is happening to me? If it's my destiny to bear children, if the womb is a precious vessel and women are assets of the nation, then someone ought to give me a medal or at least shake my hand and congratulate me on the state of grace my body has achieved.

(Oakley 1984: 16)

Menarche, and consequently menstruation, should be a positive experience. We have seen that this is far from being the case. As research by Rierden and Koff (1980) shows, high percentages of girls regarded menarche as a negative experience or a disturbing event (Whisnant and Zegans 1975).

Attitudes: reflecting ideology

The insidious influence of the ideology surrounding menstruation is reflected in the negative attitudes towards it which are held by both adolescent girls and boys. There is strong evidence that even premenarchal girls, as well as young boys, hold very negative attitudes and beliefs about menstruation (Clarke and Ruble 1978). They believe that menstruation is accompanied by physical discomforts, increased emotionality, and a disruption of social activities and interactions. What is interesting is that postmenarchal girls report that menstruation was not as terrible as they had expected it to be. However, there do not appear to be significant correlations between early negative attitudes and later experience of unpleasant menstrual symptoms. One further finding (Brooks-Gunn and Ruble 1982) was that information about menstruation learnt from male sources was identified as more negative than that derived from female sources. When asked what would be the worst aspect of being a girl, boys invariably mention menstruation. At an academic seminar on menstruation which I attended, one of the few men in the audience made the point that he couldn't imagine what it would be like to menstruate except to compare it to rectal bleeding! If this type of distortion is perpetuated at an academic level it is easy to understand why information learnt from a male source may have a more damaging effect.

Menstrual ceremonies: celebration or denigration?

In many societies the split between menstruation, sexuality and identity is not present, and it seems to be more openly acknowledged that menarche is of vital importance to the developing identity of the young woman. As Paula Weideger (1982) eloquently describes, the Apaches of North America and the Brahmins of India (amongst others) traditionally practise elaborate rituals and ceremonies at menarche. The ceremonies may involve ritual scarring, rubbing of the vulva with nettle leaves and temporary separation from the community, usually followed by a feast in celebration. These inevitably perpetuate the menstrual taboo in these cultures, and result in the adolescent girl associating her first menarche with pain and isolation. However, the concomitant celebration of fertility in these ceremonies is accompanied by a recognition of growing sexuality and an acknowledgement of the change in status which is taking place. This can act as a focus for the visible changes in the young woman's body. These ceremonies may be difficult to understand from the vantage point of Western culture, but it must be pointed out that they are no more barbaric than the practices of the Victorian doctors, or even some present-day medical interventions for 'women's problems'.

Nevertheless, the emphasis on fertility in these societies is still comparable to the close connection between womanhood and motherhood in British and American cultures, the narrow definition of a woman's role and a woman's sexuality. Only here the wall of silence surrounding developing sexuality in the woman can result in as much distress and alienation as would occur if menstrual huts were used to isolate women during the monthly period. For in our culture the women are not only isolated during the menstrual flow; much of their experience of sexuality and reproduction is split from their selves during their whole adult lives.

Silence and secrecy

It was her mother who made the fuss. Her mother who taught her to creep down from her bedroom when everyone else was asleep, to burn evidence on the fire in the dark, tiptoeing so she should not wake her father, would not have to invent a sudden thirst or hunger to explain her midnight wanderings about his house. It was imperative that he should not know. She had started wearing Tampax not for her own comfort but for the sake of more perfect secrecy. So her father should not know that the blood curse was on his house and on his possessions.

(Maitland 1981: 41)

A major part of the discourse surrounding menstruation describes it as dirty and unpleasant; concealment is of predominant importance. We can see how this is partly disseminated through advertising and teenage magazines. Menstrual products are now sold on the strength of their discretion and secrecy, with attractive floral boxes disguising the use of their contents. This capitalizes on the fact that many adolescent girls report that their greatest concern about menstruation is to conceal their sanitary products from others (Williams 1983), thus disguising the very fact of menstruation. The emphasis is on maintaining silence, not letting anyone know that you are menstruating: especially boys and men. Many women have reported that menstrual products are placed in brown paper bags by shopkeepers, as if they were on a par with pornographic magazines — something to be passed discreetly under the counter. This adds strength to the belief that menstruation is something which is dirty, and not to be discussed with anyone, family or peers.

The colloquial expressions and euphemisms surrounding menstruation maintain the negative imagery. Ernster (1975) reported that the euphemisms used between women act as a secret language, which promotes silence and secrecy: 'the curse'; 'reading a book'; 'I've come on'; or 'grandma is here'; 'the red king'; 'the red guard'; 'Aunt Emma from Reading'; 'the little visitor'; 'the package of troubles'; 'the general'; 'Bloody Mary'; 'the red road'; 'tea time'; 'the cotton bicycle'; 'red letter day'. Among males the euphemisms are often derogatory and sexual: 'in season'; 'really slick'; 'on the rag'; 'riding the rag'; 'falling off the roof'; 'she's covering the waterfront'; 'manhole covers'; 'ice-box'; 'flying the mainsail'; 'blood and sand'; 'dirt red'; 'gals at the stockyard'. This negative language, comparable to that used to describe the female genitals, is insulting and degrading to women. It suggests why information about menstruation and menarche learnt from male sources results in increased anxiety in young women.

Mothers and daughters

In our culture, and presumably in most others, the mother–daughter relationship is of central importance in the development of a woman's identity (Eichenbaum and Orbach 1983). The mother–daughter relationship is influential in the formation of the adolescent girl's perception of herself and her body. This relationship is often an ambivalent one, because the mother is usually preparing her daughter to take up a circumscribed position in a patriarchal world, similar to her own. The majority of mothers prepare their daughters for the restrictions which they themselves have lived by in order that their daughters are not misfits. This involves obedience to the social laws which define femininity: namely, deferring to others, anticipating and meeting the needs of others, as well as seeking self-definition through relationships (Orbach 1986). This may result in the adolescent girl having an ambivalent attitude towards her own body, her sexuality, and therefore her identity.

In other cultures the shared complicity of mother and daughter in the development of submissive femininity has involved rituals and rites, which irrevocably scar the daughter as a woman. The Chinese foot-binding, which produced 3-inch stubs instead of naturally grown feet, was perpetuated by mothers so that their daughters would have the sexually-valued 'lotus blossom' feet. These women could not walk unaided and suffered great pain as a result of their constraints, but could console themselves with the fact that they were attractive to men and conformed to the ideal of femininity in their culture. Female circumcision, as practised in many cultures to this day, is of the same genre. Mothers ensure that their daughters are circumcised often without adequate supervision, so that they will conform to the cultural norms for femininity and sexual attractiveness.

There has been much criticism of the interpretations which Western feminists place on the cultural practices of non-Western women, in particular female circumcision. Whilst I do not wish to enter that debate here, I do believe it is fair to draw comparisons between the practice of rituals such as circumcision in one culture and cosmetic surgery or corsets (for example) in our own.

What these customs share is the violent subjugation of women in the name of feminine beauty and enhancement of sexual desirability, permissible because of the ideology which defines a woman's worth through her attractiveness to men. The fact that the mothers are involved in this process gives fuel to those who would blame all subjugation on women themselves, saying that it is not perpetuated by the male culture but by women themselves. This argument has been applied to the physical restrictions imposed upon women, as discussed above, as well as restrictions such as the wearing of tight clothing, corsetry, impractical high shoes, etc. What it fails to recognize is the power of the patriarchal discourse and the way in which it operates. Women internalize their own oppression and become agents of their daughters' oppression. To say that women are themselves responsible for this process is facile (and of course misogynist).

How is this relevant to our discussion of sexual socialization and menarche? In the same context as that discussed above, mothers inform their daughters of the restrictions surrounding their developing sexuality, their changing bodies, and menstruation. Interviews with mothers and their daughters (Fox 1980; Bloch 1972) have shown that free discussion of menstruation and sexuality is uncomfortable, difficult, and therefore usually avoided. The mother who has been socialized in a culture which regards menstruation and female sexuality as taboo will almost inevitably pass on these attitudes to her daughter. It has been suggested (Crist and Hickenlooper 1978) that difficulties surrounding free discussion may be a result of some jealousy on the part of the mother, who is confronted with the unfolding of her daughter's sexuality. This emphasizes her own increasing age and maturity and possibly makes her envious of her daughter having freedoms and opportunities she herself missed out on. This argument suggests that the mother is challenged by her daughter's developing body, which means that many mothers find it difficult to welcome and accept the obvious physical changes which occur. In the context of the mother–daughter relationship this will be a crisis point, as the fears and worries which the mother has concerning her own body may be projected onto her daughter.

However, it is likely that mothers are socializing their daughters into accepting the bonds of femininity and motherhood from this young age because of their own internalization of the dominant ideology. To reject that ideology is to have insight into its inaccuracy and meaning, an insight which is prevented by the cloak of silence surrounding women's sexuality and reproduction.

Education devoid of reality

The inability of many young women to receive advice, information and comfort from their mothers results in their turning to other sources, such as schoolfriends and teenage magazines, for their menstrual education. These sources often reinforce the complex range of myths and taboos which both misinform and confirm the negative aspects of menstruation. For example, ideas that one should not take a bath, wash one's hair, or swim, to name but a few, are still prevalent today. An advertisement in *Jackie* magazine in February 1987 for tampons is typical of the insidious means by which these myths are transmitted:

> when you're having a period you can wear your favourite clothes, and go out to discos. You can even wear a bikini and go swimming. . . . The applicator means that you don't have to put the tampon in with your fingers . . . you'll feel confident too, because it won't smell or show.

Let us examine this material carefully, as it holds a number of implicit messages. It subtly informs the young girl of the restrictions surrounding menstruation, and tells her that they will be alleviated if she uses their product. The idea that her genitals are untouchable is transmitted by the advice about the applicator, which discourages girls from contact with their own vagina, labia and vulva. (Since it has been suggested that the plastic applicators used by many tampon manufacturers are associated with increased frequency of the Toxic Shock Syndrome[1] this encouragement of women to avoid contact with their own genitals is damaging to their physical as well as their mental health.) The final part of the advert, which suggests that the use of this product will avoid the appearance of an unpleasant smell, reinforces the belief that menstruation and female genitals are malodorous, and perpetuates those attitudes which allowed the marketing of the potentially damaging vaginal deodorants in the 1970s. In the context of such advertising it is hardly surprising that women grow up with little knowledge of their own genitals, and believe that menstruation is dirty and offensive.

How is it that these attitudes can be found in the pages of magazines in 1987? It would seem that the most basic information concerning cyclicity and the monthly menstrual flow cannot be transmitted adequately. The teaching methods, which are devoid of

35

personal and social realities, only serve to perpetuate shame and confusion. By presenting a solely physiological explanation and ignoring the social meaning of menstruation the educators are denying the fact that these women are to experience the surrounding rituals and taboos for thirty to forty years.

There also seems to be little recognition amongst educators of the importance of menarche on the development of women's self-image. Girls are more concerned with 'starting on time' and being 'average' than with biological or anatomical details. A study by Tobin-Richards *et al.* (1983), which examined pubertal events in boys and girls, found that whilst early-developing boys unequivocally enjoyed more positive body images and personal attractiveness scores than their peers, early-developing girls had lower body image scores and performed less well at school than their 'average' peers. So it would seem that the arbitrary timing of this biological event, menarche (which is predominantly dependent on body weight and health), can have a serious effect on self-image and identity. It is therefore vital that the egocentric adolescent girl, who is primarily concerned with her own normality, should be aware of the myth of the 28-day cycle, and the influence of nutrition, weight, stress, and general health on regularity of menstruation and the age of menarche (McKeever and Galloway 1984). It is important that accurate information concerning all the changes which are taking place during puberty is readily available, including changes in the distribution of weight, breast development, the growth of pubic hair, and changes in labial structure. The inability of society to provide simple, correct information has resulted in many adolescents having completely distorted ideas about what menstruation is, and therefore a fear of menarche as well as of subsequent menstrual periods. It is not uncommon, even today, to find that young girls are surprised when they realize that menstruation occurs every month, not just once. There are also many erroneous beliefs about what the appearance of blood means:

I thought my stomach was bleeding, so I didn't eat for two days in case I made it worse. We did talk about periods in school, but I thought that uterus was just another fancy name for stomach.

(J.B.)

I thought that I was suffering some sort of internal haemorrhage: that my insides were coming out. When I ran crying to my

mother, she thrust a sanitary towel and an ugly blue belt into my
hand, and told me not to make such a fuss.

(M.R.)

The importance of accurate information concerning possible
menstrual pain (dysmenorrhea) and acceptance of the existence of
this pain is also an important issue. It has traditionally been
believed that pubertal girls did not ovulate, and therefore did not
suffer from dysmenorrhea for the first six months following
menarche (Gant and McDonough 1981). However, recent research
has shown this to be an erroneous belief, as dysmenorrhea has been
found in 60 per cent of young women, with an incidence of 39 per
cent in twelve-year-olds, increasing to 72 per cent in seventeen-year-
olds (Lawlor and Davis 1981). This suggests that dysmenorrhea can
occur without ovulation. In addition, the hypothesis that any dysmenorrhea is a psychosomatic complaint, passed down from
mother to daughter, has been questioned recently, with researchers
suggesting that dysmenorrhea has a physiological base in increased
uterine contractability due to high prostaglandin levels (Klein and
Litt 1983). As McKeever points out:

The adolescent female is particularly vulnerable to assaults on
her self concept and is influenced by the opinions of others. Consequently, it is important that discomfort is taken seriously by
parents and professionals rather than being erroneously labelled
a psychosomatic or trivial complaint.

(McKeever 1984)

There is a large body of research relating to dysmenorrhea,
offering both psychological and biological hypotheses. It is not
within the scope of this book to examine this research in more
detail. What we can conclude, however, is that any adolescent girl
who experiences pain or discomfort should not be ignored or
labelled neurotic. The denial of the reality of pain will reinforce the
split between body and self, and will further impede the development of a positive image.

As I mentioned above, it would seem that the present teaching
methods surrounding menstruation are inadequate, and prevent
women from developing a positive conceptualization of their
bodies. Educational methods used in schools, where they exist at all,
are almost useless if they concentrate on biological explanations:

teaching the reproductive system of the rabbit alongside that of the human female, as if only physiology is important to us. As mothers appear to be the main transmitter of menstrual information (Fox 1980) it would seem that they should be the focus of teaching and resocializing efforts (McKeever 1984). An informed, accepting, and positive attitude towards menarche and sexual development will result in less anxiety on the part of the daughter, and less tension in the mother–daughter relationship.

The perfect body: achieving the impossible

An important theme running throughout much of the discourse concerning the adolescent girl is that of the ideal archetypal woman having a perfect body. The idea and image of the perfect female body is one which has a pervasive influence on women's consciousness and first creates conflict during puberty. Women in Western cultures are bombarded with images of 'ideal' women. An historical analysis will show us that this ideal is wholly socially constructed. The rounded contours of the Renaissance ideal contrasts sharply with the asexual flatness of the Twenties Flapper. In more recent times, the 1950s' ideal was buxom and curvacious, in contrast to the ideal a decade later, which was the almost starved appearance of the 1960s' woman. As women squeeze, constrict and pad their bodies in order to comply with some artificial ideal, they are internalizing the message that the natural body is unsightly, not attractive, and needs to be changed.

The significant messages contained in the media warn the young woman to be afraid of her body because it can let her down; by becoming fat, emitting unpleasant odours and bleeding. At the same time, she receives the message that her body is her passport to happiness: it is through her body that she entices a man, which should be her main objective. This attitude, which is instilled in adolescence, reverberates throughout a woman's life, resulting in constant worry over weight, appearance and a dissatisfaction with her body. The transformation of a body during the pubertal changes of adolescence — which conforms to society's present stereotype of feminine beauty — into one which is heavier and rounder, and therefore perceived as less attractive, causes distress for many adolescent women. It is at this stage that a major split can develop between body and self (Orbach 1986) as the young woman develops insecurities about a body which is seemingly out of control. As she looks at her changing body and compares it to the internalized norm of beauty, she is at a distance from it (Berger 1972). In the most extreme cases this sense of splitting, the loss of control, can result in anorexia nervosa. This may be the only way in which the adolescent can regain the control which she seems to have lost, to achieve the ideal, as she perceives it, of feminine beauty, the thin, boyish figure. The first menstrual period plays an important part in this illness, as the body can seem to be further out of the control of the young woman. As menstruation is symbolic of womanhood, and to some extent motherhood, this will increase the anxiety which is felt about the body. Orbach describes a woman in whom anorexia developed following the first menstrual period, for which she was unprepared. Her mother met this unexpected appearance of blood with disbelief and alarm, resulting in great feelings of shame in her daughter. The fear and resentment were projected onto her body, over which she eventually achieved control through starvation.

Jean, feeling quite odd, came to feel ashamed of this thing that was happening to her that she neither understood nor expected. She did not have the emotional vocabulary to cope with the event. She was essentially alone in the experience, with no resources to draw on. The loss of control and the fear of upset she felt were projected onto her body, which became 'out of control'. The nurse at school explained to her that she started her period so early because she was a 'big girl'. She resolved to become a smaller one and made sure that her period did not reappear for thirteen more years.

(Orbach 1986: 152)

The case of the anorexic adolescent may be an example of an extreme in a continuum, the extreme reaction to the onset of menstruation and bodily changes taking place during puberty. However, there are many young women at other points in the continuum, perhaps not attempting control over their bodies by starvation but similarly distressed and unprepared for the onset of womanhood. It is not surprising that this is the case, given the presence of damning ideology and the absence of positive constructions of the female body and reproduction within the discourse which surrounds women.

It is during adolescence that the foundations are laid which result in women being defined through their bodies, their biological structure, for the rest of their lives. We may have progressed beyond the stage of defining puberty as a form of 'mini-insanity', yet we still separate the events the young woman experiences from her self. This splitting continues throughout the life cycle, and allows the pathologizing of many of women's experiences, as they can be separated into medical entities. In this way we are no different from the Victorian physicians who blundered their way through thousands of women's lives, containing and confining. The pathologizing of the menstrual cycle is one of the most powerful ways in which women's lives are defined and dismissed through their bodies.

The discourse which describes menstruation as unclean and evidence of the weakness of a woman's body causes many women to view their sexuality as defiled, undermining their self-confidence, and the development of a positive sexual identity. Menstruation is used as a controlling factor in women's lives, with the menstruating woman identified as 'mad or bad', at the mercy of 'the constantly recurring ebb and flow of her hormones' (Dalton 1969: 4). Myths of female behaviour-change during menstruation are firmly established in our culture and internalized by women to such an extent that they often fulfil the negative prophecies by reporting disabilities which cannot be detected when objective measures are used. In the next chapter I will examine some of the evidence surrounding female behaviour and the menstrual cycle, and expose the myths for what they are.

Chapter 3

Menstruation: curse or confirmation of womanhood?

> In the old guerrilla war
> between father and son
> I am the no man's land.
> When the moon shows
> over my scorched breast
> they fire across me.
> If a bullet ricochets
> and I bleed,
> they say it is my time
> of month.
>
> (Linda Pasten, 'In the Old Guerrilla War', 1978, 15)

I have examined some of the important milestones in the development of a young woman's sexual identity, indicating ways in which the ideology surrounding reproduction and the female body affects the whole identity of the individual woman. I will now consider further the subject of menstruation. The model which I will use for my analysis of psychological research into menstruation will also be applied to pregnancy, the menopause, and the syndromes associated with these life stages in subsequent chapters.

Mad or bad? The curse of menstruation

It is impossible to form a correct opinion of the mental and physical suffering frequently endured from her sexual condition, caused by her monthly periods, which it has pleased her Heavenly Father to attach to women.

(Gunn 1924: 421)

Considering the fact that half the world's population menstruates for a significant proportion of its life, there is very little discussion of it, either in literature or in more theoretical or academic writings. The ideology surrounding menstruation — the myths and taboos which form the basis for explanations of menstruating women's behaviour — has been discussed and analysed by a small number of historians, sociologists, anthropologists and others. In general, psychologists have studied menstruation in an empirical 'scientific, objective' way, producing numerous quantitative research projects which examine minute particles of behavioural phenomena, in order to arrive at a more complete understanding of their 'subject'. They have tended to reinforce the belief that menstruation is an infirmity or a symptom of disease through research which purports to examine the reality behind the effects of cyclicity or the causal mechanisms by which the infirmity is created. Much of this research is repetitive, flawed, and meaningless: the aims and objectives of the researchers being as much in question as the methodologies which they employ.

The dominant ideology which this research supports views women's 'circulating hormones' as a liability; women are ruled by their biological make-up, which is inherently unstable. Many women, therefore, view menstruation as a 'curse' which is at best an inconvenience and at worse a debilitating illness which strikes once a month. The menstruating woman is seen as basically 'mad or bad', liable to commit crimes and prone to acts of 'lunacy'. This implies that women might spend one sixth of their reproductive lives suffering from a disabling illness which makes them unfit for many types of work, as well as for many social and sexual activities. As each woman will spend the equivalent of six years continuously menstruating, internalization of the negative constructions of menstruation can result in six years of life being deemed useless if they are not challenged. These negative social constructions of menstruation will almost certainly have a harmful effect on a woman's self-image and identity.

Taboo and silence

> The menstrual taboo is universal. . . . Generally the object of a
> taboo may be a source of good or evil, but in the case of
> menstrual blood the ascriptions are almost universally evil.
>
> (Weideger 1982: 99)

Taboos surrounding menstruation, and the associated beliefs
concerning the effects of periodic bleeding on women, seem always
to have had a pervasive influence on women's lives. Historically,
menstruating women have been isolated from the men and children
in the community, in menstrual huts or separate living quarters. In
the last century they were subjected to 'rest-cures' by the medical
profession. The taboo exists in all cultures, taking different forms
or appearances. Many separate women from the community during
menstruation to avoid contamination or contagion (Hays 1972).
Other communities avoid defilement from the menstruating
woman by isolating her from the daily contact with food or drink
which will be consumed by the men, destroying any pots or plates
that she touches (Frazer 1959). Purification ceremonies which
involve ritual baths or fumigation with smoke may take place
following the contaminating blood-loss (Hays 1972). In areas
where the menstrual taboo is very strong, a whole village may have
to be purified should a menstruating woman inadvertently pass
through. It has been known for women to be severely punished for
menstruating: in ancient Persia, women were isolated in special
rooms during their monthly blood-loss, and any woman who men-
struated for more than the four days that was deemed normal was
seen as evil incarnate:

> At the end of the four days any woman who still menstruated
> was given one hundred lashes, and sent back into seclusion for
> five more nights. At the end of this time if she continued to
> menstruate, she was given four hundred lashes because she was
> possessed by an evil spirit. Only then could the purification
> ceremonies begin.
>
> (Weideger 1982: 97)

Certain tribes of Indians would punish with death any squaw who
concealed her menstruation and then had any contact with men
who were unaware of her condition (Novak 1921). Some might
argue that such practices do not take place in Western civilization

in the late twentieth century, and that we are no longer influenced by the menstrual taboo. I would reply that the taboo remains a powerful force in our own society. Of course, it does not manifest itself in such visible ways: instead, menstruation is used to isolate women by denying or restricting them access to jobs or positions of responsibility, through the perpetuation of the belief that menstruating women are unstable. By reinforcing socially constructed, negative beliefs about gender difference, the stereotypes surrounding menstruation isolate women from men as surely as if they were shut in by menstrual huts.

In twentieth-century Western society, menstruating women are not thought liable to contaminate food or men (although the widespread avoidance of sexual intercourse during menstruation probably derives from more than dislike of blood-stained sheets). However, women are themselves perceived to be contaminated by their menstrual flow; for the archetypal menstruating (or premenstrual) woman, mood swings and depression are believed to be the norm around the time of menstruation. Women are believed to have more accidents, to be more prone to suicide, to be more likely to commit crimes, or to be admitted to a psychiatric hospital around the time of menstruation. A woman's performance, either academically or at work, is *expected* to be adversely affected by menstruation, with poor concentration and mood changes creating an unstable and irrational employee.

Research has shown that both men and women believe most of these stereotypes about the menstruating woman, although most women report that other women are much more severely affected than themselves (Brooks *et al.* 1977). This suggests that it is cultural stereotypes rather than real experiences which form the basis for these beliefs. By defining women as dirty, dangerous and unstable, these stereotypes strengthen the belief that the reproductive capacity of our bodies is a handicap. In our modern 'scientific' society it is not the magical or spiritual qualities of the menstruating woman which are emphasized, but the hormonal imbalances which are somehow measurable and therefore more real: 'people thought that there was something magic or evil about menstrual blood. Now we *know* that it's chemistry that's doing the damage. We're clumsy and accident-prone because the chemical balance of our bodies is upset' [my emphasis] (Kingston 1980: 26). Scientific 'evidence' has been produced to support these claims, based on the assumption that women are ruled by their hormones, and the objective of scientific enquiry has merely been to identify the actual mechanisms by which this operates.

The premenstrual syndrome: an insidious influence in all woman's lives

The premenstrual syndrome, by all accounts, is uncomfortable, miserable and isolating — and brings out the worst side in all of us.

(Shreeve 1984: 35)

In twentieth-century society the connection between the womb, the reproductive system, and a woman's madness has been legitimized and elevated to the status of scientific knowledge, largely through the creation of the premenstrual syndrome. In her 'self-help' manual, Caroline Shreeve, who, it is stressed, is 'an experienced doctor', calls the premenstrual syndrome 'the curse that can be cured'. This epitomizes the value-laden, negative conceptualization of menstrual-cycle variabilities, which are medicalized through being interpreted by someone who is 'qualified to give practical and sympathetic advice'. Whilst this description, which is typical of most texts on the menstrual cycle, is both patronizing and glib, it also serves to place knowledge and control of women's bodies firmly in the hands of the experts, the doctors; those who claim to be rational and unbiased.

The premenstrual syndrome provides scientific legitimacy for the traditional 'raging-hormone' theories. As it assumes the status of a 'known' illness, a syndrome, it gives scientific backing to discrimination against women. Yet the validity of this syndrome is totally questionable and close examination of its discovery exposes the fragile foundations on which it is based.

Premenstrual tension (PMT) was first described by Frank (1931), who labelled a cluster of feelings (including tension, unrest, irritability, and hostility) as 'premenstrual tension' due to the fact that they regularly occurred in the days preceding menstruation. In more recent years the term 'premenstrual syndrome' (PMS) has gained widespread use, mainly because researchers pointed out that changes which were being recorded in the premenstrual phase encompassed experiences much more wide-reaching than 'tension'.

The premenstrual syndrome is now a 'recognized' psychiatric illness in the eyes of many practitioners and researchers, alongside schizophrenia, manic depression, etc. It was recently put forward for inclusion in DSM IV (the diagnostic and statistical manual of the American Psychiatric Association), which would constitute the official recognition as a diagnostic category. Interestingly it has not been accepted, despite the arguments of many eminent psychiatrists — perhaps partly due to the vociferous feminist lobby which challenged its inclusion as a syndrome. Yet PMS has replaced the theories of the 'hysterical womb' and the contaminated blood to account for behaviour in a large number of perimenstrual women.

It has been suggested (Laws 1985) that PMT has been renamed PMS because of the former term's 'bad name'. Laws compares this to the renaming of Long Kesh prison in Northern Ireland ('The Maze'), and the renaming of Windscale nuclear power plant ('Sellafield'). This analogy highlights the political implications of the existence of a categorical term to describe this aspect of women's experience. I believe that the renaming was mainly carried out to provide scientific validity for the description of cyclical change as illness. The medicalization, renaming and general mystification of cyclical phenomena have served to isolate women from their own experiences, placing control in the hands of the self-proclaimed experts — the doctors and the drug companies — who attempt to define reality. Some women have claimed that PMS is a preferable term to use as it has removed the emphasis on tension and allows for positive aspects of cyclical change to be monitored. Yet surely such benefits are far outweighed by the knowledge that large numbers of women are described as suffering from a monthly psychiatric syndrome, within the description of PMS as a psychiatric disorder.

> At least 40 per cent of women who menstruate have some degree of PMS; about 10 per cent have severe problems with it. PMS is also, probably, an unhelpful hidden factor in many more women's lives: accidents, poor performance and anti-social behaviour are markedly more common in women just before menstruation.
>
> (Swaffield 1987: 24)

This purports to be a factual statement in a recent, fairly sympathetic, article on PMS. Its author presumably believed that she was reporting the scientific evidence, not merely a number of minor, methodologically flawed research studies (which happen to support the dominant ideology and thus are frequently quoted: see below p. 58). This shows the pervasive influence of the research on PMS, or at least one form of it, on the discourses concerning women.

Let us now examine the scientific evidence for PMS and the way it is used to define women as ruled by their hormones. I will use the term PMS rather than PMT since it is the description of cyclical change as part of a syndrome which is the most pervasive amongst doctors and researchers, and which has the most damaging implications for women.

What then exactly is this syndrome, PMS, which 'experts' say affects between 5 per cent and 95 per cent of women (Harrison *et al.* 1985), depending on the definitions which they use and the specific population studied? Definitions of the syndrome have ranged from 'the recurrence of any symptoms always at the same time in each menstrual cycle' (Dalton 1964) to combinations of over 150 symptoms including back pain, elation, depression, sexual desire and tension (Moos 1969). More recent researchers have described PMS as a constellation of 'affective and physical changes' which occur in the luteal phase (the second half) of most cycles, with relief from symptoms at the onset of menstruation and at least one week of symptom-free intervals. The ambiguity concerning the 'symptoms' of PMS has led to a comparison with other 'imitators' in the history of medicine, such as syphilis or tuberculosis, where symptoms have been ascribed to the disorders without it being established that they are in fact related (Notman and Nadelson 1979). We can also see that the symptoms are strikingly similar to those of hysteria and neurasthenia, those epidemics which struck nineteenth-century women in similar proportions.

Despite such large estimates of suffering there is still much disagreement over the diagnosis and aetiology of PMS. It is peculiar that a syndrome over which there is no agreed diagnosis can be said to affect so many women: are we discussing the same 'illness' here at all? As there are no agreed criteria for diagnosis, self-diagnosis is often used as a means by which to define women as 'sufferers' or 'non-sufferers'. It has been reported (Van den Akker 1985) that a high percentage of women attending a clinic for PMS were indistinguishable from a 'non-suffering' control group of women, suggesting that subjective reports of PMS cannot act as a basis for 'diagnosis'. In my own research (Ussher 1987) no difference could be found, on psychological or behavioural measures, between a group of women who reported severe PMS and a group who claimed to be asymptomatic. Abraham *et al.* (1985) suggest that as the same cyclical symptoms can be found in women who complain of PMS and those who don't, women should not be used in research studies as 'PMS sufferers' unless some agreed, objective criteria are fulfilled. If women should not be used in research studies on this basis, is it not *more* important that they should not be subjected to 'treatment' regimes that often have harmful side-effects? Since the 'objective criteria' on which to base a diagnosis remain speculative at present, the continued use of PMS as a diagnostic category is clearly dubious.

Suggestions put forward by the 'experts' for the aetiology of PMS are a further cause of controversy. They are all, almost without exception, internal attributions of aetiology, ranging from the hormonal fluctuations discussed below (p. 49) to personality factors, individual differences such as age or religion, or a myriad of 'psychological' factors. I will list these in order to show both the wide range of different theories and the lack of coherence between the researchers. For a more complete discussion of these theories, interested readers should see the reviews of this subject.[1]

Biochemical aetiological suggestions have included imbalances or deficiency in the following:

Female sex hormones	Frank 1931
Estrogen progesterone	Morton *et al.* 1953; Smith 1975
Water retention	Dunnigan 1983
Altered activity of the cortex	MacKinnon and MacKinnon 1956
Plasma monoamine oxidase activity	Klaiber *et al.* 1974; Belmaker *et al.* 1974
Renin–angiotension–aldosterone	Janowsky *et al.* 1973
Prolactin–progesterone interaction	Benedek-Jazmann and Hearn-Sturtevart 1976
Pyridoxine deficiency	Rose 1969; Winston 1973; Herzberg *et al.* 1970; Brush 1977

Gonadotrophin imbalances	Backstrom 1975
Peptide hormones (i.e. endophines, endogenous opiates, and encephalins)	Grossman *et al.* 1982; Butt *et al.* 1983; Halbreich and Endicott 1981; Reid and Yen 1981
Prostaglandin effects	Craig 1980; Jakubowicz 1983
Sodium–potassium	Varma 1983
Dopamine action	Haspels 1983

This wide-ranging array of hormonal 'causes' for the supposed syndrome has resulted in a large number of hormones being used to treat women with PMS. However, as it is established that there is a placebo effect of between 20–80 per cent (Sampson 1979; Taylor 1983), the reports of effective biochemical treatments must be viewed with caution. In addition, there is a paucity of controlled studies of treatment efficacy, with many methodological problems such as small samples, lack of controls, few double-blind or cross-over studies, inadequate definition of PMS, and poor control of variables such as medication.

Biochemical treatments include:

Oestrogens	Shaw 1983
Progesterone	Dalton 1969; Kerr 1977
Diuretics	O'Brien *et al.* 1979
Monoamine oxidase inhibitors and Bromocriptine	Benedek-Jazmann and Hearn-Sturtevart 1976
Lithium	Mattson and von Schoultz 1974; Singer *et al.* 1974; Horrobin *et al.* 1973
Oral contraceptives	Herzberg *et al.* 1970
Pyridoxine	Abraham and Hargrove 1980
Prostaglandin antagonists and precursors	Puolakka and Makarainen 1985; Wood and Jakubowicz 1980
Dygesterone	Varma 1983

The lack of agreement amongst researchers concerning hormonal aetiologies and treatment efficacy has led to the suggestion that factors other than the biochemical are involved. Psychologists have proposed many aetiological theories, ranging from an analysis of the role of psychiatric disturbance to the role of attitudes. It is interesting that for nearly every study which purports to show a relationship between menstrual-cycle complaints and a psychological construct, there is a second study which disputes this. This shows that no firm conclusions have been reached by psychologists, despite the claims of some. I will list some of the theories below, to give an idea of the type of hypotheses which have been put forward. (For a more complete analysis of these see Asso (1983).)

Psychological theories of PMS include:

Rejection of femininity	Deutch 1944; Patkai and Peterson 1975; Levitt and Lubin 1967
Acceptance of femininity	Paige 1973; Gough 1975
Embarrassed mother	Slade and Jenner 1979
Locus of control	Scott-Palmer and Skevington 1981
Expectations	Rodin 1976
Negative attitude to the body	Dinardo 1974
Anxious personality	Halbreich and Kas 1977
Neuroticism	Gruba and Rohrbaugh 1975; Rees 1953; Coppen and Kessel 1963
Life stress	Clare 1983; Siegal *et al.* 1979
Marital problems	Sampson 1979
Changes in arousal	Asso 1982; Little and Zahn 1974
Attribution of arousal	Koeske 1977
Emotional instability	Sheldrake and Cormack 1976; Levitt and Lubin 1967
Psychiatric disturbance	McClure *et al.* 1971 (and numerous others)
Attitude	Woods *et al.* 1982; Dennerstein *et al.* 1982

As well as examining theories of aetiology, psychologists have tried to analyse the exact cyclical variations which women experience, concentrating on examinations of performance, behaviour and mood, in order to clarify exactly how menstruation affects women's behaviour.

A woman's prerogative

'Women do suddenly change their minds in a way that men don't. . . . Their moods can change suddenly, and hormones may be responsible. The word 'hysteria' literally means a condition caused by the womb and 'lunacy' refers to the monthly cycle'.

(Dalton 1981)

Changes in mood during the menstrual cycle, with negative moods being experienced during the menstrual or premenstrual phases, are assumed to take place in almost all women, which has led to the definition of a large proportion of women as PMS sufferers. These supposed mood changes are seen as being at the root of many behavioural variations which are said to occur, such as the supposed increased propensity of women to commit crimes, have accidents or fail at their work, theories which we will examine later in this chapter. The theory that a majority of women suffer from cyclical mood change has been put forward as the evidence for the widespread existence of PMS. Many authors and researchers use the evidence of any cyclical mood change to represent the existence of PMS in individual women. This, again, supports the ideology which defines women as unstable and ruled by their hormones.

It is a central part of the stereotype of the menstruating woman that she is moody, irrational and unreliable, either premenstrually or during menstruation. Yet there is remarkably little empirical evidence for this. In terms of the psychological research, the picture is inconclusive: some studies report that women do experience more negative moods premenstrually,[2] others that such moods occur in the menstrual phase of the cycle,[3] and others no cyclical variation at all.[4] Most of the research concentrates on negative aspects of cyclicity, using questionnaires which only contain the opportunity for responses to negative symptoms.[5] It is not surprising that women only report negative feelings, such as depression or anxiety, if those are the only feelings which are being investigated. As more recent research has shown, perhaps unsurprisingly, that women do experience positive moods at every stage of the menstrual cycle,[6] many of the biased research studies are being challenged. Women themselves report different degrees of cyclical mood change:

> I always feel angry or on edge, liable to let loose when my period is due. It's almost as if everything I've been refusing to acknowledge for weeks comes rushing forward to grab me.
>
> (Joanne)

> I always seem to have so much energy around the time of my period: I can finish my work in double quick time, then cook a meal for friends without feeling tired. It's as if I can't sit still.
>
> (Jean)

> The best description of the way I feel just before I come on is like a flower which has just opened up its petals to the world: I feel sensitive and peaceful, as if nothing could disturb my sense of tranquillity.
>
> (Denise)

> Menstruation: I don't think that it affects me at all. I only remember that I'm due to start bleeding by looking at my diary, certainly not by any changes in me.
>
> (Evette)

These reports, from women whom I interviewed for my own research, support the contention that there is no one mood profile which can possibly account for the experiences of the majority of women. Women cannot be lumped together as if a homogeneous group, with identical experiences.

One interesting piece of information which the research studies record is that there is a marked difference between women's retrospective accounts of cyclical mood variations, their memories of mood in the preceding month, and their concurrent or daily mood reports. It is generally found that women report marked cyclicity in mood — with negative moods experienced premenstrually — when asked to account retrospectively, but that this pattern is rarely observed in daily ratings (Abplanalp 1983). There have been several suggestions to account for this discrepancy. One is that women may be fulfilling cultural stereotypes with their negative social expectations when completing retrospective questionnaires. Thus the internalization of the belief that women are prone to cyclical mood change affects women's perception of their own cyclicity.

In an interesting study which supports this theory (Ruble 1977), women's beliefs about which stage of the cycle they were in were manipulated; they were variously informed that they were either premenstrual or intermenstrual when they were at the same stage (six to seven days before menstruation). The 'as if premenstrual' group reported a higher degree of stereotypically appropriate negative symptoms than the 'as if intermenstrual' group. Ruble interprets this as evidence of the influence of psycho-social factors on the reporting of menstrual distress. It could also be the result of expectations based on experiences, yet none of the women reported particularly severe symptoms.

A further issue which confounds the results of many of the experimental studies is the suggestion that women may be picking out particular aspects of mood to report, as they know that the menstrual cycle is the subject of study.[7]

Arousal and activation: possible explanation for feelings?

It has been suggested that an explanation for the inconsistent findings of the research studies, and the varying reports of women themselves, may be found in a study of arousal or activation during the menstrual cycle, coupled with an analysis of attributions and expectations. One common aspect of different reports of any menstrual variability in mood seems to be a premenstrual increase in activation: the underlying level of physiological state. This can be interpreted by individual women in different ways:

It's as if I'm a spring that has been wound up so far, until I can't wind up any more: then I let the tension out by crying or shouting — and sometimes even by laughing!

(Jane)

I always feel closer to the edge when I'm premenstrual: as if I can do anything I want to do — and sometimes I end up doing and saying things I didn't intend to at all. It feels like a tremendous energy, that is potentially really destructive, but can be constructive.

(Isabel)

There is a body of research which suggests that there are underlying physiological changes in activation or arousal taking place during the menstrual cycle, which may be interpreted by women in different ways and therefore account for the finding that some women report menstrual cycle mood change whilst others do not. Although the concept of arousal is not without problems, it is of some use to us as a construct which may provide an explanation for individual women's experiences. While I will not consider the research into activation and the menstrual cycle in any detail here, there are several excellent reviews which suggest that although the results are not unequivocal, there is a strong likelihood that autonomic activation increases during the premenstrual phase of the cycle (Asso and Braier 1982).

One might ask how this is relevant to my task of exposing the stereotype and presenting an alternative way of understanding menstrual cycle distress. The activation theorists, if we may name them collectively, provide the biological/physiological evidence for an integrated theory which examines women's constructions of their experience, based largely on those constructions prevalent within the culture.

The way in which the physical changes in activation are interpreted and thus experienced is not a straightforward biological relationship, as would be suggested by the raging-hormones theory, but a complicated interaction of social constructions, attributions of the individual and socio-political factors. This theory has its foundation in the original work of Schacter and Singer (1962), who increased the activation of subjects in an experimental setting and then presented them with either positive or negative situations. This showed that the increased arousal could be experienced either positively or negatively, depending on the context and the expectations of the subjects.

It has been argued that the attribution of perceived state change during the menstrual cycle can have a marked effect on mood and behaviour. Randi Koeske (1977; 1980) has argued that negative moods, 'symptoms', and behaviours, which occur in the premenstrual phase of the cycle, are likely to be attributed to biological factors; whilst positive moods, 'symptoms', and behaviours are likely to be attributed to personality or situational factors. Therefore, women who feel depressed or irritable premenstrually are likely to blame their premenstrual state for the mood change, whereas if they feel positive or happy they are likely to attribute this to situational factors, produced by generally held beliefs and expectations.[8] These differential attributions will result in only negative symptoms being labelled as cyclical, and reinforce the negative attitudes which women have towards their bodies and their sexuality, since their bodies are associated only with negative or debilitating factors.

In an attempt to explain why some women report positive moods premenstrually, Parlee (1981), agreeing with the non-specific arousal theory, stated that positive moods which are reported in the premenstrual phase are a result of the interpretation of non-specific arousal in a positive way, due to favourable or satisfactory life circumstances. Thus Parlee suggests that women who have a more problematic or stressful life, and have internalized the ideology of a problematic menstruation, may be more likely to call premenstrual state changes 'depression'. Where their life is good and positive, women may interpret their arousal in a positive fashion, even if they do attribute it to outside events.

In Koeske's study there were also indications that male anger and female pleasantness in an upsetting situation are judged as acceptable, whereas female anger was deemed unacceptable (Koeske 1977). This supports our argument (see p. 72) that labelling such unacceptable, out-of-role behaviour as part of a 'syndrome', giving it a diagnostic category, provides a social explanation for women's discontent. Otherwise it is incongruent with the stereotype of woman in our society.

These theories seem to me to be the most relevant produced by psychologists so far. They provide some explanation for why there are so many individual differences between the experiences of women, and are a means of understanding women's distress without relying on internal pathological explanations. They also provide hope for positive interventions for individual women who experience distress, for women can work within an attributional framework to reassess their lives and their symptoms, as I will argue in the final chapter.

Stress: increasing vulnerability?

A number of studies have suggested that menstrual distress is directly related to negative life events. In my own research there was a stronger relationship between negative moods and symptoms and life events than between these moods and cycle phase. These daily life events were evaluated and defined by the women themselves and varied from:

I laddered my tights on the way to work.

I missed the bus on the way home and had to walk for a mile.

to:

My husband heard yesterday that he was to be made redundant.

One of the children has developed whooping cough.

These particular events above, which are representative of the responses I obtained, include both everyday occurrences and the major established life events (equivalent to marriage, divorce, moving house, bereavement etc.), which have been shown to be related to psychological distress. These life events or stresses which I examined in this small goup of women were of importance to them, and seemed to be significantly related to their mood. It has in fact been suggested (Clare 1983) that the finding that women do not complain of negative premenstrual symptoms in every cycle may be largely a result of monthly changes in social circumstances.

There are a number of other studies which have related PMS or menstrual distress to major life stresses, such as marital problems (Siegal *et al.* 1979). At the other end of the spectrum, it has been suggested (Rossi and Rossi 1977) that the day of the week may be more important in determining mood state than menstrual cycle phase, with a low point on Tuesday and a high point on Friday! Abplanalp (1983) suggested that if the day of the week is a more important indicator of mood than cycle phase, then some women must be more susceptible to negative moods on a Tuesday, when they occur premenstrually, as vulnerability may be increased.

A shift to understanding PMS in terms of stress supports the contention that women are experiencing distress during the menstrual cycle as a normal reaction to life circumstances, or to oppression. Yet because of the unavailability of appropriate channels within which women's distress can be expressed, unhappiness is pathologized and dismissed as illness, located within the individual woman. If women cannot express their unhappiness or frustration, which occurs as a result of socio-political factors, without challenging the stereotypical view of woman, they will learn to express their unhappiness in a culturally acceptable way; that is as a syndrome which can be cured. As a result, all women can be dismissed as moody, irrational, and unreliable; and who wants to employ an unreliable worker?

Women's performance: fluctuating wildly, or constant and reliable?

We cannot too emphatically urge the importance of regarding these monthly returns as periods of ill health, as days when the ordinary occupations are to be suspended or modified. . . . Long walks, dancing, shopping, riding, and parties should be avoided at this time of month invariably and under all circumstances.

(Taylor 1871: 284–5)

It is an indisputable, if regrettable, fact that if you suffer from premenstrual syndrome, you are likely to work less efficiently for a few days each month, and that your poorer powers of concentration and reduced memory ability will inevitably affect your overall efficiency.

(Shreeve 1984: 78)

Two comments, made one hundred years apart, both give out the same message: women are unreliable workers because of their monthly cycles, which result in infirmity, inefficiency, and ill health. So in addition to changes in mood during the cycle, which can be attributed to underlying pathology and act to dismiss women as unreliable, the dominant ideology also construes women as being untrustworthy employees, because their performance fluctuates with the moon. One of the questions which psychologists have asked is whether performance or behaviour really do vary during the menstrual cycle.

A variety of functions, ranging from simple perceptual judgements to the use of complex cognitive processes, has been studied in relation to menstrual cycle performance, in both experimental and natural settings. Overall, laboratory studies of performance, or studies of performance in a work situation, tend to show no consistent variations across menstrual cycle phase, despite the cultural stereotype of the woman at the mercy 'of the ebb and flow of her hormones' (Dalton 1969), reflected in the negative expectations of many women.

The results of the existing research must be considered with some caution, due to the many methodological problems involved and the varying complexity of performance tests employed, as well as doubts concerning the appropriateness of generalizing the results to everyday life. There is, however, some validity in considering the experimental paradigm, as it has allowed us to examine quite subtle relationships between performance and cycle phase. The results of the experiments also support the contention that the dominant belief that menstruation is debilitating is a myth, not based on reality.

Performance in the workplace

Performance has been examined directly in the workplace in an attempt to see whether menstruation affects performance in a real life situation.[9] Much of this type of research has been carried out to serve the needs of industry. As Sayers (1982) points out, it is interesting that the results that were being published during the Second World War (i.e., Seward 1944), when women were a vital part of the industrial workforce, proclaimed that menstruation had no debilitating effect on women's output. In our present economic climate the results more likely to be published are those (few) which show a premenstrual performance decline. 'The cost to industry of menstrual problems is measured in millions of pounds, liras, kroners or dollars, not in terms of human misery, unhappiness or pain' (Dalton, quoted in Sayers 1982: 122). Yet despite current attempts to confine women to the home, as unemployment is high and the prevailing ideology advocates a return to family values, there is no evidence to suggest that the effects of menstruation on performance can be used to support this move.

Any positivistic research purporting to show a relationship between menstruation and performance is often eagerly embraced by the prevailing socio-economic interests and we can be sure that if such evidence did exist, it would be well publicized. One conclusion reached by a reviewer of this subject was that menstrual absenteeism is the result of suggestion, since withdrawing pay for leave taken as a result of menstrual problems dramatically reduced the level of absenteeism (Seward 1944)! This is good evidence of the narrow-mindedness of some of the researchers, who seem to be unaware of the realities of life for many women, and naïvely believe that menstruation can be studied in isolation.

Athletic performance

There are also studies of athletic performance during the menstrual cycle, which I mention here as sport too can be classified as a real life situation. As with the industrial performance studies, there is no evidence to suggest that menstruation has any effect on athletic performance.[10]

Analyses of the performance of swimmers, basketball players and Olympic athletes all produce the same results: menstruation has little or no effect on women athletes' ability to train or compete. The only group of athletes who felt that menstruation was an issue were swimmers, who were less likely than other groups to train during menstruation. This is probably a result of the internalization of the old belief that women should not swim during, or immediately preceding, menstruation, rather than because of any differences between groups of athletes, for modern sanitary protection would ensure that there was no need for these swimmers to cease participation in their sport during menstruation.

Experimental performance testing

The majority of research investigating performance and the menstrual cycle has been carried out in the laboratory using experimental settings which can be easily controlled by the psychologist. One might say cynically that the reason for the proliferation of this type of research is the apparent ease with which the two variables of performance and menstrual-cycle phase can be compared — it makes a nicely designed study. In fact menstrual-cycle phase is often included in analyses alongside other independent variables, such as age or sex, as if it were completely unproblematic. We need to question the motivation of the researchers who carry out this work. I would argue that they do it for little more than self interest, to obtain research publications or a degree. The majority of this research is of no use to women, either in providing a greater understanding of cyclicity, or in being applicable to real life situations.

Many of the studies examine one discrete aspect of performance (such as reaction time, patellar reflex, or verbal fluency), correlate performance with menstrual cycle phase and then jump to conclusions about women's general performance capability throughout the whole cycle. I will not go into detail about the myriad studies which exist; there are a number of reviews which interested readers could obtain (Sommer 1983; Graham 1980; Asso 1983). What is needed here is an overview, and a suggestion of how this research can be understood in the context of the other information on the menstrual cycle.

The general conclusion of the numerous research papers on the subject is that there is no evidence for a cyclical variation in performance, either on cognitive or psychomotor tests. In a review of forty-eight tests used to measure menstrual variations in performance, Sommer (1983) concluded that thirty-five show no phase effects. This is in accordance with an earlier review by the same author (Sommer 1973), and a review by Graham (1980). Those few studies which do report a significant relationship use single tests or subtests, and can often not be replicated. As one would expect 20 per cent of results to be significant by chance (at the 0.5 level) it is not surprising that a few studies will report a significant relationship between menstruation and performance, where there is in fact no relationship. I would argue that most of the research which uses single tests and which cannot be replicated should be disregarded, because of the many methodological problems and the knowledge that research using batteries of tests shows no relationship between menstrual cycle phase and performance.

Academic performance

All heavy exercise should be omitted during the menstrual week . . . a girl should not only retire earlier at this time, but ought to stay out of school from one to three days as the case may be, resting the mind and taking extra hours of rest and sleep.

(Scott-Hall 1916: 202)

The idea that women's academic performance is affected by their 'raging hormones', or, conversely, that their reproductive functions will be damaged by education as mentioned in Chapter 1, has been a hotly contested issue for several years. Should girls taking examinations be allowed dispensation because they are menstruating? One of the most quoted pieces of research was carried out by Katrina Dalton (1960a), who studied the examination performance of schoolgirls aged eleven to seventeen years, and reported that there was evidence of a performance decrement in the menstrual and premenstrual phases. However, this research may have been misinterpreted by many people, as the actual percentages are: 56 per cent of girls showed no change over the cycle; 17 per cent showed an improvement, and only 21 per cent showed an impairment. Added to the fact that there was no attempt to analyse these results statistically, there seems to be little basis on which to claim a cycle phase effect.

In a follow-up study, Dalton (1968) claimed that there was evidence of menstrual cycle impairment on O and A level examination results. The average mark was 3 per cent lower for menstruating subjects, the pass rate 13 per cent lower and the distinction rate 9 per cent lower. However, as Sommer (1983) points out, there were great methodological problems in this study. In the A level examinations, the grades were analysed from 180 papers submitted by 34 subjects; in the O level examinations, 162 papers from 91 individuals were examined: which puts a disproportionate weight on subjects submitting more than one paper. In the analysis, a between-group comparison was being made between those in one phase, with those in another: these results are not based on the same person at different phases of the cycle, and differences between the two groups are possibly confounding variables. In this study, a disproportionate number of girls were menstruating from the number one would expect by chance. As Dalton states that stress of examinations brought about a change in cycle in 42 per cent of girls in the study, it would seem erroneous to claim that menstruation brought about any change in academic performance, even if that could be proven, because a third factor, such as stress, may be at the root of any change observed.

A number of studies have looked at the academic performance of American college women during the menstrual cycle (Bernstein 1977). One of the criticisms of much of modern psychology is that it is really the psychology of American psychology students, who are nearly always the subjects of experiments. So it is not surprising that we have a number of studies of American undergraduates' performance during the menstrual cycle. Yet the results of this research reinforce the argument that there is no relationship between menstruation and academic performance.[11]

As we can see, there has been a considerable amount of empirical research into the question of menstrual cycle variations in mood and performance. One could say that it is becoming a standard undergraduate psychology project, with each new study producing much the same results. It is an interesting phenomenon to examine: why do women researchers (as the majority of these researchers are women) seem to need to prove that there is no effect of menstruation on behaviour? I myself undertook three years of research to 'prove' this fact. Do we, as women, need to validate our beliefs, challenging the ideology which damns us, through the adoption of the scientific method of research? Perhaps it is because non-significant results are rarely published (only 3 per cent of published studies report non-significant results (Smart 1963)) and the work of these many women remains unknown. In the eyes of the scientific community, therefore, it does not exist. There must be an alternative way of creating our own discourse, challenging the stereotypes and producing an alternative explanation to the pathological medical one, for problems which women experience.

Yet mood and performance changes are not the only variables which psychologists have studied in order to find a menstrual cycle effect on behaviour: accidents, hospital admissions and crimes have all been analysed, in order to ascertain whether the mad/bad archetype of the menstruating woman has any basis in reality.

Accidents

> The best ways of travelling to work if you are suffering from premenstrual symptoms are either to walk, if it's not too far, or to obtain a lift. Cycling, riding a motorbike, or driving are not choice means of transport at a time when you are likely to be slow and clumsy, and accident prone.
>
> (Shreeve 1984: 74)

It has been suggested that women are more likely to have accidents in the menstrual or premenstrual phase of the cycle, which Shreeve's self-help guide takes as fact. This reinforces the stereotype that women are unreliable and untrustworthy because of their bodies.

One of the most quoted findings is that women aeroplane pilots are more likely to crash whilst menstruating. Obviously if one generalizes from this women are not to be trusted in responsible positions, especially where there is some risk to life. In fact, women were denied their pilots' licences in the 1930s on the basis of this claim. However, as Parlee (1973) points out, the only evidence for the increased vulnerability of women pilots is from a study by Whitehead (1934), which reports three aeroplane crashes in three months, in which the women were *said* to be menstruating at the time of the crashes. The original author does not authenticate his claim with any information as to how this was established nor does he provide any information as to the overall total number of crashes which occurred, from which he was extracting his menstruating sample. This 'fact' looks like fantasy.

Other research carried out to look at accidents in the menstrual cycle is similarly flawed, and gives further evidence of the way in which spurious findings are published and advertised because of their support for the dominant ideology.

In a review of the research in this area, Katrina Dalton (1964), the most enthusiastic proponent of the raging-hormones theory, concluded that there was evidence for an increase in home and road accidents in the menstrual and premenstrual phases of the cycle. As an example, in a study of accident admissions to hospital, Dalton (1960b) reported that over 50 per cent of a sample of eighty-four women were in the premenstrual or menstrual phase of the cycle. Increased lethargy, associated with hormonal change, is suggested as the underlying cause of the accident increase. However, there was no objective measure of this supposed increased lethargy. A further suggestion is that accidents may be to do with quarrels, which could be caused by premenstrual tension. A study by Lees (1965), using 1000 subjects, supported Dalton's findings, reporting a higher proportion of accidents in the menstrual and premenstrual phase of the cycle. However, MacKinnon and MacKinnon (1956) reported a *low* frequency of accidents in the menstrual phase of the cycle.

Women's behaviour can be explained in terms of their raging hormones even when they are dead (and thus unable to challenge this diagnosis). MacKinnon *et al.* (1959) used the analysis of female uteri, carried out at autopsies, to determine phase of cycle of women who had died from accidents or suicide. Of 58 women studied, 6 died in the bleeding and follicular phase of the cycle, and 52 in the postovulatory stages, with 34 of these in the mid-luteal phase. The authors interpret this finding as evidence for an increase in serious accidents in the second half of the cycle. Yet this analysis has many flaws, as we shall see below.

Menstrual madness: psychiatric hospital admissions

> Bertha's madness is . . . linked to female sexuality and the
> periodicity of the menstrual cycle. Her worst attacks come when
> the moon is 'blood red' . . . or 'broad and red'; at these
> moments she is vicious and destructive, although at other times
> she is lucid and calm . . . a prisoner of her reproductive cycle.
>
> (Showalter 1987: 67)

Elaine Showalter, above, discusses the madwoman Bertha
Rochester, a character from Charlotte Brontë's *Jane Eyre* (1847),
whose madness was tied to menstruation. This particular stereotype
has been investigated by psychologists, with unsurprisingly
equivocal results. Their purpose has been to examine the suggestion
that there is an increase in psychiatric hospital admissions and
suicide attempts during the menstrual and premenstrual phases of
the cycle, a suggestion which coincides with the archetype of the
menstruating woman as mad (and/or bad). This theory confirms
the belief that women's minds are intimately connected to their
wombs and that the monthly blood flow unhinges women, making
it impossible for them to be rational. If we accept that women are
more likely to suffer from psychiatric disturbance premenstrually,
we are accepting it as one end of a continuum, in which any woman
can be dismissed as disturbed or unbalanced, and liable to psychiatric disturbance.

What is the evidence from the research studies to suggest that
psychiatric admission is greater during the menstrual or premenstrual phases of the cycle? There are arguments that hospital admission is greater in the menstrual phase of the cycle: Katrina Dalton
(1959) reported that 39 per cent of acute hospital admissions
occurred during the first four days of menstruation, in contrast to
an expected admission rate of 14 per cent by chance. However, the
14 per cent admission rate during the premenstrual period was no
greater than expected. Luggin *et al.* (1984) investigated the acute
psychiatric admission of 121 women, and found that significantly
more women were admitted during the menstrual phase than the
intermenstrual phase of the cycle. It has also been claimed that
women are more likely to phone a suicide prevention centre in the
menstrual phase of the cycle (Mandell and Mandell 1967). Yet these
findings contrast with those of MacKinnon and MacKinnon (1956)
who found a *low* frequency of accidents in the bleeding phase.

This is typical of research in the area of the menstrual cycle, where almost any finding can be juxtaposed with an opposing one, providing an inconclusive picture.

Other studies have claimed to show that hospital admissions or suicides are greater in the premenstrual phase of the cycle. For example, Glass *et al.* (1971) studied emergency psychiatric admissions and attempted suicides in eighty-four women, and reported that twice as many as were expected were seen in the emergency room in the premenstrual phase, with three times as many as expected suicide attempts occurring in this phase. A study of attempted suicides by Tonks *et al.* (1968), in which it was reported that there were significantly more in the premenstrual phase of the cycle, also contained the finding that there were significantly more suicide attempts made by women living with men!

One problem with this research is that the authors fail to mention that menstrual bleeding may be affected by the stress of psychiatric disturbance, or by the life stresses that precipitated the suicide attempt. Most of these studies are correlational in nature; those who do show a significant relationship are merely reporting positive correlations between menstruation and a behavioural index. The influence of a third variable, such as stress, is not considered. As it has been established that menstruation is affected by stress (Dalton 1960b; Dunbar 1985), with stressful life events possibly precipitating menstrual bleeding, the relationship between menstruation and accidents or illness may be chance, as both may be determined by a third variable. Yet these considerations are not taken into account by those who use the research findings to reinforce their belief that insanity and menstruation are linked.

Motherhood in question

Many children do get injured, not necessarily by a drunken father or a fighting mother, but at times by a parent (in this case let's say a premenstrual mum) who suddenly snaps, and hits out before she is able to control herself.

(Shreeve 1984: 93)

One of the more insidious theories or suppositions about the effect of menstruation on a woman is that it affects her ability to be a 'good mother'. This suggests that not only are women unfit to work, or make major decisions; because of their unreliability and irrationality they are also unfit to be mothers.

The quote above suggests that a woman may find herself harming her child because of PMS. It has also been suggested that a woman's menstruation affects her perception of her child's health. In a study of women attending a general practitioner for the treatment of minor ailments in their children (Dalton 1966), it was reported that 54 per cent of the women were in the premenstrual or menstrual phase of the cycle, compared with an expected 29 per cent by chance. In a further study (Tuch 1975) of ninety-five women attending a hospital paediatric department with their children, 51 per cent were found to be in the menstrual or premenstrual phase, compared to an expected 39 per cent. The mothers of both groups (perimenstrual and non perimenstrual) viewed their children as equally ill, yet the doctors viewed the children of the perimenstrual group as less ill.

The implication of these studies is that worrying about one's child or judgements about illness may be related to the menstrual cycle, which produces a lack of self-confidence. If this is so it is likely to be a result of women's internalization of the stereotype that menstruating women are unreliable, rather than because menstruating women lack clear judgement. The findings are worrying, as they could be used to question a woman's ability to be a 'good' mother at this time in her cycle, suggesting that she has become neurotic and untrustworthy. Ignoring a mother's fears and worries about her child is a common failing in the medical profession today, resulting in anxiety and resentment in the mother as well as the loss of a rich and usually accurate source of information. One could argue that if there were some evidence to suggest that mothers bring their children to the doctor more readily in the perimenstrual phase of the cycle, this shows that they might be more perceptive in this phase, and possibly more aware of discomfort in the child. However, there are so few studies published which support this finding that its reliability must remain uncertain.

Jekyll and Hyde: criminal behaviour and violence

Recent court cases in which women, independently, have used premenstrual distress as a defence for crimes of violence, only serve to confirm the stereotyped view that women are more violent, or more likely to engage in criminal acts, in the premenstrual or menstrual phases of their cycles. In November 1981 Christine English was tried and acquitted for manslaughter, on the grounds of diminished responsibility due to PMT; 'a woman whose premenstrual tension turned her into a "raging animal" was freed [after] threatening police with a knife' (The *Sun*, 11 November 1981).

In a more recent case, reported in the newspapers on 23 April 1988, Anne Reynolds was freed from court after having 'battered her mother to death after having a secret love child' (*Daily Mirror*). This case is more worrying, as PMT and postnatal depression (PND) seem to be being considered as the same entity: both reinforcing the idea that women are inherently dangerous and unstable. Under the banner headline 'Girl, 19, who murdered her mother was suffering from PMT, say judges', it was reported: 'at the time of the killing, Anne Reynolds, 19, had been suffering from PMT — premenstrual tension — and depression after the birth of her baby' (The *Daily Mirror*, 23 April 1988). We cannot know from this type of newspaper reporting whether the judges were more specific in their understanding, distinguishing between PMT and PND, or whether *any* hormonal imbalance was thought to be the same thing. What is obvious is that the newspaper is not distinguishing between the two syndromes: women's raging hormones are thought to be at the root of the violent behaviour, whether premenstrually or post-natally. This reinforces the stereotype of woman as a Jekyll and Hyde character, who may commit violent criminal acts as a result of hormonal fluctuations. 'There is mounting medical evidence to show that at certain times of the month, and for no other reasons, some women can go berserk' (The *Daily Mirror*, 11 November 1981).

What is this mounting evidence? As with many areas of menstrual cycle research, the findings are sparse and inconclusive. In one study, Dalton (1960b) reported that 49 per cent of crimes (in contrast with an expected 29 per cent), committed by a group of 156 female prisoners, were perpetrated during the premenstrual or menstrual periods. Dalton attributed this effect to hormonal changes which increase lethargy and tension and thereby increase the chance of being caught. A second study, carried out by Morton *et al.* (1953) examined a group of female prison inmates, and reported that 62 per cent of violent crimes committed by women took place during the premenstrual week, 19 per cent midcycle, and

17 per cent during menstruation. However, the authors do not define the lengths of each of these latter two cycle phases, nor do they state how they defined cycle phase at the time of the crime. Most of the women studied in this type of research were required to recall the stage of cycle they were at when committing crimes many months, or even years, before. It is doubtful that they would be able to remember this accurately. In addition, eight of the fifty-eight women in Morton's study were in a 'don't remember' category, which casts doubt on the rest of the findings. Women may be fulfilling cultural expectations when retrospectively recalling cycle phase: believing that they were in the premenstrual phase when committing a crime fits in with the stereotype, and may seem to the women to provide a legitimate explanation for their crime.

The way in which research findings are inaccurately interpreted is evidenced by the way in which a study by Cooke (1945) is cited by many authors as proof of a relationship between crime and the menstrual cycle (Greene and Dalton (1953); Coppen and Kessel (1963); Morton *et al.* (1953); MacKinnon and MacKinnon (1956)). However, as Parlee (1973) points out, the only evidence put forward by Cooke is a statement by the Parisian police, to the effect that 84 per cent of crimes by women are committed in the premenstrual or menstrual phases of the cycle: no other substantial evidence or reason for this claim is offered.

Reports of the acquittal of Christine English (see p. 67), on the grounds that her violence towards her lover which resulted in his death was mediated by her hormones, may well be being used in the same manner as the spurious study by Cooke. For despite the fact that an appeal judge, Lord Justice Griffiths, ruled that 'PMT (is) wholly unacceptable as a defence to any crime' (27 April 1982), there is now a legal precedent to provide 'objective' evidence that women may become violent as a result of menstruation. This may have been the reason behind the description of Anne Reynold's crime in 1988 as being due to PMT, despite the fact that depression following the birth of a baby was given as the cause for her behaviour. The use of PMT as an excuse for women's violence has been accepted by society, by the popular press, and thus makes easily digestible news.

The archetypal image of women in our society does not include the capability or motivation to carry out violent crime. In the case of Christine English there was ample evidence for provocation, in the form of violence from her lover accompanied by his boasts of his other women. Were the defendant a man, this provocation would have almost certainly been used as a defence — and may have resulted in acquittal — as in the recent cases of men acquitted of killing their wives on grounds of provocation. However, within the confines of the female role, women are not allowed to express anger or to be violent, therefore hormonal interpretations of behaviour offer acceptable explanations. As Valerie Hey (1985) points out, 'Women's non-feminine actions are more likely to be interpreted by a medical model because we cannot accept that women commit such acts for very much the same reasons as men'.

This is extremely damaging for women, for hormonal explanations pathologize women, negating any legitimate expression of anger which women might voice, as well as suggesting that they are out of control.

The premenstrual syndrome: a mythical construct disguising oppression

I have now come full cycle: this chapter began with a description of the madness, badness, or recurrent illness model of menstruation, which is legitimated and consolidated within the concept of PMS. The implications of this model for women's lives can now be seen, thus bringing us back to an analysis of the syndrome, PMS. It is not merely of theoretical interest to examine the ideologies of reproduction, to examine how women are conceptualized as unreliable, 'faulty vessels' through the construction of the female body as weak, dangerous, and somehow a greater determinant of women's behaviour than men's bodies are of theirs. These ideologies have real effects on women's lives, both through the 'interior colonization' (Millett 1971) by which women accept the labels attached to them and experience their bodies and reproductive cycles as debilitating, and through the way in which these ideas of women are woven into the whole fabric of our society. The legitimating of the ideology, through the development and widespread acceptance of the concept of the premenstrual syndrome, will result in women being controlled, dismissed, and tied to their biology, in the same way as the hysteric or the neurasthenic were in the past.

Premenstrual changes — the concept of the premenstrual

syndrome — cannot be understood outside the social and political context of women's lives. As Laws (1985) reports, the social construction of premenstrual changes as part of a negative and debilitating syndrome only serves to perpetuate the idea that women are 'at the mercy of the ebb and flow of their hormones', and reinforces the continuing inequality of men and women in the workplace and in the home. It has been shown that there is little empirical evidence that women's performance suffers during the paramenstruum, little evidence to support the idea of the accident-prone, unstable, potentially mad, menstruating woman. Yet the myth persists; it is repeatedly said that 'evidence' exists and thus damaging and inaccurate images of women and of the female body are perpetuated.

What I am challenging is the concept of immutable, biological, pregiven categories, in which the female body is seen as a fixed entity which will influence women in a predetermined way. The idea that women are closer to nature than men and are influenced by their hormones presupposes a biological blueprint which women cannot change or adapt.

Yet I am not suggesting that we ignore biology, that we ignore women's reproductive cycles, in favour of a solely social-constructionist argument, as many feminists have suggested we should. For as Rich notes:

> female biology — the diffuse, intense sensuality radiating out from the clitoris, breasts, uterus, vagina; the lunar cyles of menstruation; the gestation and fruition of life which can take place in the female body — has far more radical implications than we have yet come to appreciate. Patriarchal thought has limited female biology to its own narrow specifications. The feminist vision has recoiled from female biology for these reasons; it will, I believe, come to view our physicality as a resource rather than a destiny.
>
> (Rich 1986: 39)

The dualism between biological determinism and social constructionism often results in a less than complete understanding of women's experiences, ignoring important aspects of women's lives. To deny the effects of biology completely is to ignore an important factor, and does not serve to counteract biological determinism, because the effects of biology are not examined. In order to address these issues, a number of theorists have argued that we must examine the *interaction* between biology and socially constructed categories in order to come to a complete understanding of the individual in society. However, Henriques *et al.* (1984) suggest that this 'leaves the idea of an unmediated biology unchallenged'. Thus theorists who argue that menstruation, for example, is largely experienced as a socially constructed category, are not challenging those who argue that there are some aspects of menstruation which are pre-given categories.

> whilst we should avoid founding a theory of subjectivity on a taken-for-granted biological origin, we cannot construct a position which altogether denies biology any effects. The only way to this without granting either term of the biology–society couple the status of pre-given categories is to reconceptualise them in such a way that the implicit dualism is dissolved in favour of stressing the relational character of their mutual effects.
>
> (Henriques *et al.* 1984: 21)

This means that we cannot work solely within the dichotomy of a biological given or a social construct, weighing up the influence of each of these factors and determining which is the most important in influencing behaviour or experience (or dismissing one altogether). Categories which we may assume are biological givens or social constructions may not be straightforwardly either, but the result of a complex relationship of many different factors. Women's experience of menstruation, as of pregnancy and the menopause, is both biological and social. No factor can be considered in isolation from the rest and no factor is a pre-given category that will have a consistent and predictable influence.

Premenstrual changes as a 'syndrome': a misnomer with dangerous influence

With this in mind, the validity of the concept of a 'premenstrual syndrome' must be questioned. Whilst we must recognize that a number of women do suffer from distressing symptoms premenstrually, the labelling of these symptoms as a syndrome is inappropriate, since each individual woman's 'symptom' profile may be different. This has resulted in the description of a syndrome which potentially has 150 different symptoms, which may occur in any combination. It is also important to acknowledge the discrepancies in the literature and the lack of agreement between different researchers and clinicians as to the correct 'objective' diagnosis of PMS. The distressing feelings reported by a number of women are not immutably related to their hormones, and cannot be understood within a simple causal model.

Before expanding on this it is necessary to examine the validity of using the concept of syndrome to describe premenstrual experiences of women. One major difficulty in defining any set of symptoms as a syndrome is whether a syndrome is constituted by a fixed group of symptoms or can be represented by a common but not invariant set of symptoms (Walsh 1985). In the case of the menstrual cycle, the latter would have to be the case, since there are so many individual differences between women. This use of the term 'syndrome' infers that the symptoms concerned have a greater concordance among themselves than each has with other symptoms, with statistical analysis confirming the strength of the interrelationships (Walsh 1985). This could not be said to be the case with the possible symptoms found in the premenstrual syndrome, as many are part of other diagnosed syndromes, such as anxiety or depression, in similar groupings.

It has been suggested (Kinsbourne 1971) that not all 'ingredients' of a syndrome have equal importance, which creates uncertainty as to which symptoms have to be present to justify diagnosis. There is, as yet, no agreement concerning the essential features of a premenstrual syndrome, for surely it is inadequate to suggest that any constellation of symptoms, providing they occur cyclically, may be diagnosed as part of a premenstrual syndrome. If the term syndrome is used in such a broad way, it fails to have any meaning. Even the proviso that the symptoms must increase premenstrually to constitute a syndrome may be a questionable concept, as recall of symptoms has been shown to be different when recorded retrospectively or daily. This suggests that attitudes, stereotypes and/or the effects of 'internal colonization', are affecting many women as memories. The use of the concept of PMS in the general population to describe moderate cyclical mood change may result in women being labelled 'ill' for a significant number of days each month, resulting in further discrimination and sexual divisions in society. The move to include PMS as a recognized syndrome in the latest additions to DSM IV (see the *BPS Bulletin*, April 1986), as discussed earlier, suggests that women who report any cyclical mood change may be defined as suffering from a psychiatric disorder which recurs every month. As a syndrome suggests an underlying disease process (Walsh 1985), the implications for women's self-images may be extremely serious.

Femininity as pathology

The paradox, that women who conform rigidly to the female role model as well as those who unambiguously reject it are likely to be labelled psychiatrically ill, is one we cannot ignore. Broverman *et al.* (1970) showed how cultural stereotypes of the female and male role models were accepted and internalized by mental health professionals of various disciplines and were used in the evaluation and diagnosis of mental health problems. The definition of a healthy adult, either male or female, conformed to the masculine stereotype, whilst the feminine stereotype, of passivity, conformity, less aggression, lower achievement motivation, etc. was seen as psychologically unhealthy. However, adult women were generally seen as:

> more submissive, less independent, less adventurous, more easily influenced, less aggressive, less competitive, more excitable in minor crises, having their feelings more easily hurt, more conceited about their appearance, [and] less objective.
>
> (Broverman *et al.* 1970)

Recent work has shown that mental health professionals still adopt these stereotyped views of what is normal and healthy for women, which undoubtedly influence their diagnosis of mental health 'problems'. Women who conform to the cultural norms of femininity are likely to be defined as psychologically unhealthy, as are men who exhibit feminine characteristics. Paradoxically, of course, women who *reject* the female role are equally likely to be labelled as deviant, and given a psychiatric diagnosis. 'What we consider "madness", whether it appears in women or in men, is either the acting out of the devalued female role model or the total or partial rejection of one's sex role stereotype' (Chesler 1972). Women who are adventurous, competitive, sexually active, independent, who reject the role of wife and mother — to name but a few examples — may all be designated psychiatrically ill. Many of the 'symptoms' of the premenstrual syndrome involve aspects of female behaviour which society defines as deviant in women: this includes anger, moodiness, emotional instability, tiredness, violence, increased/decreased libido. It would seem that PMS provides an excellent explanation for this out-of-role behaviour, and now that it is on the way to receiving the status of a psychiatric syndrome, this behaviour can be seen as pathological.

Defining aspects of behaviour which may vary with the menstrual cycle as 'symptoms' or arranging them within a diagnostic category or a conceptual framework, allows them to be construed as a 'distinct entity', which can then be perceived as causing the symptoms in the first place (Penfold and Walker 1984). In this way women are seen as patients, whose behaviour, feelings, or thoughts are dismissed because of their 'diagnosis'.

> once a person is suspected or diagnosed as mentally ill, she becomes someone who is not expected to make sense in terms of the social definition of rationality or normality. She is also not to be related to in the same way as someone who is not mentally ill, and what she says is not given the same credence.
>
> (Penfold and Walker 1984: 42)

The premenstrual syndrome simultaneously explains and dismisses a great deal of women's behaviour. It defines cyclical change as pathological, when in fact predictability of any mood or behaviour could be beneficial. Perhaps it is time that women themselves spoke out about menstrual cycle variabilities. This is beginning to happen, but has still not permeated popular consciousness. We do not need cyclical change to be defined as an illness: there are many women who experience positive cyclical change, and many others who may only express their true anger or frustration with life at the time of the month when it is more culturally acceptable to do so.

The minority of women who seem to suffer from debilitating moods or experiences premenstrually may not be helped in the short term by a critical analysis of PMS, as it could appear to be dismissing their experiences. However, if menstrual cycle changes were not seen as pathological but as a normal part of the female experience, then it would be easier for women who need support to receive it. The biological occurrence of menstruation does not inevitably condemn women to suffer or to be weak; it is through a complex process that women experience the menstrual cycle as a curse. A reconceptualization of this biological entity, which is not pre-given in its influence, would have dramatic effect:

> The best cure is to stop calling it premenstrual tension. Call it PME — premenstrual energy — instead. Energy suggests a gift. . . . 'Tension' implies that you're stuck with it. 'Energy' suggests it can be released, and in a creative fashion at that.
>
> (M. Grace Melucci, *Ms*, 5, 1982)

The psychological research which has been carried out to investigate the menstrual cycle can provide valuable information to those who are attempting to come to a greater understanding of the female life cycle. It shows how the myths and stereotypes of the 'mad or bad' menstruating woman are erroneous, whilst at the same time providing indications for positive interventions, which I will discuss in the final chapter. The influence of stressful life events, as well as the importance of the attribution of causation, may provide a valuable framework for the understanding of why some women report premenstrual problems.

Yet much of the psychological literature in the positivistic tradition is based on a scientific rhetoric which is at odds with our desire to liberate women from the confines of a pathological model. It has also been used to support the ideology which confines and frames women, rather than being used to help us repossess our bodies. The pathological model is also used as an explanation for the distress experienced by women at critical stages in their life cycle, notably pregnancy, childbirth and the menopause. The myth of motherhood, and the existence of the syndrome of postnatal depression, as we shall see, are as much based on inaccurate stereotypes and ideological illusions as the myth of the mad/bad menstruating woman.

Chapter 4

Pregnancy and motherhood: malady or mourning?

> the Almighty, in creating the female sex, [took] the uterus and built up a woman around it.
>
> (1870 doctor: quoted in Smith-Rosenberg and Rosenberg 1973: 335)

Childbirth is (or may be) one aspect of the entire process of a woman's life, beginning with her own expulsion from her mother's body, her own sensual suckling or being held by a woman, through her earliest sensations of clitoral eroticism and of the vulva as a source of pleasure, her growing sense of her own body and its strengths, her masturbation, her menses, her physical relationship to nature and to other human beings, her first and subsequent orgasmic experiences with another's body, her conception, pregnancy, to the moment of first holding her child. But that moment is still only a point in the process if we conceive it not according to patriarchal ideas of childbirth as a kind of production, but as part of female experience.

(Rich 1986: 182)

Pregnancy, childbirth, and motherhood are an intrinsic part of women's experience, regardless of whether or not we decide to give birth to children. These experiences need to be seen in the context of the whole life cycle and of the dominant beliefs surrounding the female body, which act to frame women from the cradle to the grave.

A growing number of writers, including sociologists, historians, anthropologists, and psychologists, are producing a body of literature examining the effects of pregnancy, childbirth, and motherhood upon women. They have attempted to identify the mechanisms by which motherhood contributes to women's subordination, identifying 'myths of motherhood' and the discourse through which mothering is constructed, as well as showing the depersonalization of the individual woman, who is stripped of power during childbearing and childrearing. Graham and Oakley (1981) have eloquently dissected and criticized the role of the medical profession in this depersonalization; a process which we can examine and understand as being part of the same process which medicalizes and pathologizes women's distress at other stages in the life cycle — such as during the menstrual cycle or during the menopause.

The way in which pregnancy and childbirth are construed in our society contributes towards the constriction of women's lives, producing women as carers and nurturers, rather than as achievers or providers. The majority of the psychological research which has been carried out to investigate pregnancy and childbirth maintains the idea of women as natural mothers, reinforcing the myth of motherhood. Psychologists have tended to concentrate on 'deviant' aspects of pregnancy, such as factors involved in nausea and vomiting (Macy 1986), marital problems during the transition to parenthood (Moss *et al.* 1986) or psychiatric problems experienced during or immediately following pregnancy (Kendell *et al.* 1981). This work, which looks to the individual psychology of the pregnant woman to explain her 'abnormal' reactions, reinforces the notion of pregnancy as an illness, as well as perpetuating the link between a woman's reproductive functioning and her behaviour, the raging-hormones theory which frames women throughout the life cycle. As pregnancy and motherhood are mainly divorced from other aspects of that experience, such as menstruation or the menopause, as the common connectedness of these experiences is rarely discussed, women are prevented from making connections which may challenge the dominant ideology, and a further splitting of body and mind is perpetuated.

Mothers confined: oppression through the ages

The woman's body, with its potential for gestating forth and nourishing new life, has been through the ages a field of contradictions: a space invested with power, and an acute vulnerability; a numinous figure and the incarnation of evil; a hoard of ambivalences, most of which have worked to disqualify women from the collective act of defining culture.

(Rich 1986: 102)

The combination of ideology and ignorance surrounding pregnancy and birth has worked to isolate women from this central part of our lives for centuries. In the Western world until the fifteenth century, birth was primarily the concern of women, and men were excluded from the scene of labour. Female midwives, later relabelled witches, provided solace and support, guiding the woman through labour and birth, often with the aid of herbal painkillers. This arena of power was not unchallenged by the male medical profession, who declared that the field of obstetrics was primitive and unchanging because of the ignorance of the women midwives. From the fifteenth century onwards the men took over, turning the art of the wise women and witches into a scientific practice, which employed tools such as forceps, and from which women were barred. The recent film *Dead Ringers* (Cronenberg 1989) is both a grotesque celebration and a parody of this fact.

From the late nineteenth century onwards the 'science of motherhood' has developed and flourished, as psychologists and other self-proclaimed 'experts' on the condition of pregnancy and childbirth have sought to apply their positivistic empiricism to the science of reproduction. An understanding of female psychology was felt to be essential for the medical profession, the obstetricians who controlled and cared for women during pregnancy and childbirth; and this notion of female psychology has been used to maintain the notion that women are weak and potentially volatile during reproductive 'crises', of which pregnancy is the primary one. As one obstetrician, much influenced by psychoanalytic ways of thinking, proclaimed:

regression in the course of pregnancy is universal and normal, and pregnancy has aptly been called a 'normal illness' . . . just as the regression of the pregnant woman brings to the surface childhood fears, so we find the pregnant woman as suggestible as a child.

(Heiman 1965: 480–1)

As psychologists looked to problems within the internal pathology of the woman — problems in adjustment to the female role — as a means of explanation for menstrual-cycle distress, women who expressed discontent during or following pregnancy were understood in terms of their rejection of femininity (Benedek 1963), somehow suggesting that they were not 'real women'.

> The very fact that a woman cannot tolerate pregnancy, or is in intense conflict about it, or about giving birth to a child, is an indication that the pre-pregnant personality of this woman was immature and in that sense can be labelled as psychopathological . . . pregnancy and birth are the overt proofs of femininity . . . [and to these women] receptivity in the feminine role appears as debasing. . . . Pregnancy as a challenge of femininity is unacceptable to them.
>
> (Fromm 1967: 210)

Problems with female role adjustment have also been postulated as an explanation of nausea during pregnancy. Yet the original much-quoted paper which discusses this theory is not based on any substantial evidence. In fact, as Macy (1986) observes, this supposition is based on little more than a throwaway remark. Much of the psychological research is of a similar genre to that carried out to investigate the menstrual cycle: *ad hoc* explanations with no theoretical basis for the research.

Within the confines of this book I cannot examine all of the psychological literature on pregnancy or childbirth; I will thus concentrate on the effects of pregnancy and childbirth on women's identity. I shall examine the work of feminist psychologists such as Paula Nicolson (1988) and consider some of the ways in which pregnancy and childbirth have been socially constructed within the ideological framework which defines women's experiences. Pregnancy and childbirth are important life events for women, yet they are often viewed in isolation, not as a part of the whole life cycle, making women often feel alone, adrift: 'Birth is a major life event, and for many of us a crisis . . . like a tiny boat at sea without sight of land, caught in a cross current, with wave upon wave crashing (Kitzinger 1987: 1). Pregnancy, birth and the transition to motherhood will undoubtedly have considerable effects on identity: yet pregnancy is rarely discussed by identity theorists, or those who examine development throughout the lifespan. If it is, it is in the context of transition to parenthood, rather than as an examination of the effects of pregnancy, birth, or motherhood on the woman. Could this be because the general transition to parenthood affects men, and is therefore of more interest to male researchers, than the state of pregnancy?

Pregnancy: a time of change

Being a woman is synonymous with being a mother, because of the 'central importance of "mother" within female identity' which results in an 'ideological symmetry between "woman" and "mother"' (Nicolson 1988). Becoming pregnant and becoming a mother are seen as providing status for women, supposedly a positive identity, a sense of achievement, and for many, adult status. Becoming a mother is seen to be every woman's crowning glory, the pinnacle of her achievement: what we are all destined for, and ultimately the only means of true fulfilment. Even today, when effective methods of contraception give women more choice, most of us express a desire to have children; studies of adolescents reveal that the majority express a desire to combine career and motherhood (Becket 1986). The women who declare that they don't wish to become mothers are seen as deviant.

It is difficult for women to separate the potential to bear children from the image of self, whether or not we decide to have children. For women who choose not to have children (or are unable to have children) are labelled and defined by the state of childlessness, as much as women who do have children are defined by their status as mother. Motherhood is an integral part of our identity as women, even in this 'post-feminist' world of sophisticated reproductive technologies and highly effective methods of birth control in which women have supposedly been freed from their reproductive chains. Once a woman becomes a mother, she has accepted this role for life. Society will define her through her status as mother — even as a prime minister — much more than men are ever defined through their status as father. 'This is an exceptional case. You have shown yourself to be a good wife, a good mother and a good housewife and I cannot think of anything more one could say about any woman' (Justice Boreman, quoted in Adams and Laurikietis 1976: 113).

Thus pregnancy is undeniably a significant life event for women, with the birth of the first child heralding a complete change in life circumstances and life style, including relationships with significant others and changes in occupational status. Each additional child will also have a considerable effect on a woman's life, on her view of herself: it is not merely the first which has an impact and effects change (Nicolson 1988). A recent study (Condon 1987) has suggested that greater depression is experienced by multiparous women during pregnancy, possibly due to the strains of caring for a young child whilst being pregnant.

One of the most significant changes, and one which is often ignored by those who produce best-selling books on pregnancy and childbirth, is the change in identity. The often contradictory discourses concerning pregnancy and motherhood frequently result in an identity crisis for individual women, as a split occurs between identity as a person, a single unit, and identity as a mother. For example, it has been suggested that a sharp conflict occurs between a woman's cultural femininity, which requires dependent and inactive behaviour, and her biological femininity, which demands aggression, activity and competence.

The first pregnancy implies the end of the woman as a single unit, and the beginning of the mother–child relationship. Although many theorists would argue that it is birth itself and the concomitant changes following birth which are the significant factors in a woman's life, changes in identity are taking place from the beginning of pregnancy. Therefore we should examine the continuum of change from the start of pregnancy through to the experience of becoming a mother. A woman begins to assume the identity of mother in the eyes of society almost as soon as she is visibly pregnant, ceasing to be a single unit long before the birth of her child. This change in a woman's status and identity is frequently beset with difficulties and anxieties, problems which most women are not prepared for by their idealized expectations. As Oakley (1986) notes:

> while the predominant cultural myth of motherhood states that giving birth to, and being able to look after, a baby, is an achievement of a peculiarly feminine and beneficial kind, it was obvious from what women in the study said that childbearing and childrearing commonly possess quite profound qualities of loss for the woman herself.
>
> (Oakley 1986: 208)

This is the loss of identity as an autonomous person, which will be replaced by the identity of 'expectant mother' then 'mother'. This role transition is not always an easy one, however, for the paradox by which women gain a socially acceptable identity as mothers, whilst simultaneously experiencing a loss of self, is one which leaves many women confused and depressed. This ultimate goal of motherhood is not necessarily a positive experience, for as Woollett (1987) notes: 'Becoming a mother demonstrates a woman's success as a woman, as well as in reproductive terms: yet much of what mothers do is unsatisfactory, tiring, isolating and socially devalued.' And, as Ann Oakley points out, 'It is hard to avoid the fact that there is something really depressing about motherhood' (Oakley 1986: 61).

Paula Nicolson (1988) has argued that one way in which women are oppressed by motherhood is through not being allowed to mourn or grieve their lost sense of self. To experience sadness at the annihilation of self is surely a necessary response, given the patriarchal framework within which the majority of women experience motherhood. Women feel that they have to make a choice between motherhood and individuation, motherhood and creativity, motherhood and freedom (Rich 1986); it is thus unsurprising that a sense of sadness or loss prevails. Yet through the perpetuation of ideology and the myth of motherhood, society expects that the pregnant woman, or the new mother, will be happy and glowing. Women generally compare themselves to what they perceive to be the ideal mother, or the ideal expectant mother, accepting the dominant ideology and often finding that their experience is not synonymous with that. Their position within the contradictory discourses of creative/free woman versus mother is untenable, and therefore women often experience feelings of conflict and unease, which are labelled depression. Either during pregnancy: 'Drained of all vitality, smelly, with a tinny taste in my mouth, I wondered where this much vaunted pregnancy radiancy was. I felt ghastly!' (Kitzinger 1983: 199). Or following childbirth: 'I couldn't seem to do anything right: I felt so tired, the baby kept crying, and I kept thinking that this was supposed to be the most fulfilling experience of my whole life. It felt like the most lonely, miserable experience' (Lesley, 3 weeks after the birth of her first child).

The images of the 'ideal mother' who nurtures selflessly (Chodorow 1978) and is always competently in control, and that of the 'super-mum' who can effortlessly manage house, children, a full-time job, and the demands of her partner (and who loves her children continuously), are the standards against which women evaluate themselves. There is little or no preparation for the reality of motherhood, the contradictory feelings, or the ambivalence:

> Throughout pregnancy and nursing, women are urged to relax, to mime the serenity of madonnas. No one mentions the psychic crisis of bearing a first child, the excitation of long buried feelings about one's own mother, the sense of confused power and powerlessness, of being taken over on the one hand and of touching new physical and psychic potentialities on the other, a heightened sensibility which can be exhilarating, bewildering and exhausting. No one mentions the strangeness of attraction — which can be as singleminded as the early days of a love affair.
>
> (Rich 1986: 36)

The archetype of the serene madonna, juxtaposed with the capable super-mum, is constantly promoted and reinforced by the agents of socialization: the media, education, and, in this case, the medical profession. It is little wonder that many women are disheartened by a reality which is far from the ideal and that they experience a sense of failure. This perpetuation of the fantasy of the ideal mother has led to women being culturally oppressed in order that the needs of children will be met: yet those very needs are also the product of fantasy.

I am not arguing that pregnancy, childbirth, and motherhood are inevitably negative or depressing experiences. A number of women express increased emotional well-being during pregnancy, but they do appear to be in the minority: one study suggesting fewer than 15 per cent of women (Condon 1987). There are women who find fulfilment through this role, who express joy at their newly-born child, who find the transition to motherhood an easy one. For these women who do not contradict the stereotype, the expression of their feelings is easy — society will welcome their joy as confirmation of the belief that women are destined to be mothers and can only be happy through doing so. These women are lucky: for many women who have internalized society's construction of motherhood as the ultimate fulfilment for a woman — 'society's golden carrot' (Comer 1976) — it is difficult to express their 'dysfunctional' feelings. These contradict what women expect to experience, in direct opposition to the archetype of the joyous madonna. 'Motherhood wasn't what I had expected — unadulterated wonder. The shock of the isolation and much of the sheer slog and boredom were exacerbated by the fact that I felt I wasn't supposed to feel dissatisfied' (Wandor 1980: 136).

For many women the stereotypes of the joyous pregnant woman who has never looked so beautiful and the radiant/serene, fulfilled mother often have little basis in fact. Increased anxiety, tiredness and physical discomfort have been reported in many pregnant women (Elliot 1984) and women who have recently given birth (Nicolson 1988). These feelings of depression during the course of pregnancy have also been reported by expectant fathers (Condon 1987), suggesting that it is the psycho-social changes which are important, rather than any internal biochemical changes.

Many women feel ill at ease with their new status as mother, experiencing loss of identity, yet cannot fit these feelings into their conceptualization of being a 'good mother'. Thus they come to understand their experiences as an illness, which has been labelled postnatal depression or 'the baby blues'. A similar process may be operating with the 'depression' that is experienced by large numbers of pregnant women, for they are also prevented from expressing discontent easily because of the pervasive influence of the 'myth of motherhood':

> Brenda . . . keeps her feelings bottled up and feels she must not (in case her mother would be upset) or cannot (in the case of friends who would not understand, and Mike who would only blame her) reveal her depression, unhappiness concerning the marriage and panic about labour.
>
> (Case study, Rossan 1987b: 3)

The myth prevents analysis of the contradictory positions of women inside the cultural framework through which we con-ceptualize reproduction. The feelings of unhappiness experienced by many women following childbirth are labelled abnormal because they do not fit in with the discourse of the woman as a joyful, instinctual, and competent mother. Rather than looking for an explanation in the socio-political context of mothering, these symptoms are assigned a clinical label and become pathologized. The guilt and resentment which this can result in for individual women can only exacerbate an already difficult situation:

full-time mothers, struggling to keep a home spotless and tidy, know what it is to resent, and fleetingly hate, an infant or a pre-schooler as if it were a full-grown adult adversary. If mother-hood was 'fulfilment' then these flashes of hostility must be traitorous, and implicitly destructive of all that was normal, good and decent. Science could not account for these feelings except as perversions — serpents in the Eden of the mother–child relationship. The result was agonising self-doubt: the mother who is blamed for her 'hostility', her 'aggressiveness' and also . . . for disguising it, is a mother whose own internal life has been rendered inhuman and unintelligible. As her own wants and needs are interpreted as destructive toxins, she drifts towards actual psychosis.

(Ehrenreich and English 1979: 205)

The same process occurs with the premenstrual syndrome, as we have seen in Chapter 3: assigning a clinical label to this 'depression' both explains feelings and symptoms, whilst simultaneously being seen as the cause of those symptoms. The description of women's feelings of unhappiness following childbirth as 'postnatal depres-sion' (PND), or 'the baby blues' reinforces the idea that such women are to be treated as 'faulty machines', dysfunctional women who fail to achieve a 'correct' response to motherhood. Through using pathological explanations we avoid examining the nature of the oppression which women experience as mothers. We have neat syndromes which compartmentalize women's experiences through the use of a disease model, identifying internal causes for their unhappiness. This defines women as ill and thereby dismisses their unhappiness and prevents an analysis of why it is occurring.

Postnatal depression: pathologizing distress after childbirth

Postnatal depression seems to have become the blanket term used by many practitioners to explain all female discontent in the period following the birth of a child. It has: 'virtually transcended the state at which it needs to be defined or explained, and thus, *despite lack of evidence*, has become an accepted part of female life' (Nicolson 1988: 66, my emphasis). In a review of a recent text of postnatal stress, Sandra Elliot (1987) criticizes the author for referring to 'psychoses, blues, early onset depression and late onset depression . . . under one label, PND'. Yet there is a distinct lack of clarity as to the distinguishing features of each of these different syndromes or classifications: perhaps one could argue that this is to ensure the inclusion of any symptoms experienced after childbirth under a convenient diagnostic label.

The 'baby blues' are usually distinguished by their fleeting nature, lasting for a matter of days (sometimes weeks) and confined to the early postnatal period. The symptoms include 'elation, emotional lability, depersonalisation and confusion' (Elliot 1984: 96), and are found in a majority of women following childbirth.

'Postnatal depression', a clinical disorder, is said to affect between 3 and 25 per cent of women (Elliot 1984), the estimate depending on the methodology used by the researchers. It is difficult to give a description of the symptoms of postnatal depression, as there is little agreement between different researchers and practitioners. Although a number of women are undoubtedly depressed following the birth of a child, recent reports have questioned whether this depression is different from that experienced at any other stage of the life cycle (Bennett 1981). Elliot (1984) has suggested that a continuum, as opposed to the dichotomy of depressed/not depressed, is more relevant as a model of understanding. This would allow for a description of each individual woman's physical and emotional experiences, without the label of 'normal' or 'depressed' needing to be attached. This model would seem to be more applicable to the analysis in this book, yet it is still purely descriptive, and does not attempt to provide explanations for the distress experienced by women.

I do not want to appear as culpable as the author reviewed by Elliot (above) in failing to distinguish between different types of depression after childbirth. Yet I will use the term PND in this discussion as it is this which is most widely used by both 'experts' and lay people, and which thus has the greatest potential of becoming accepted as a real syndrome, an actual clinical entity. In addition, as a descriptive entity, PND is closely aligned to PMS (as we have seen in the newspaper reporting, discussed on p. 67) and thus can be conceptualized in a similar way.

We can draw many comparisons between PMS and PND (not least their reductive acronyms). First, there is little evidence for the existence of PND as a discrete entity. As we have seen with PMS, researchers and practitioners find it difficult to isolate exact criteria for diagnosis while different diagnostic criteria are used by different researchers, often to suit the needs of their own study rather than in an attempt to understand the phenomena. Second, there is a temporal factor associated with both PMS and PND, which are supposed to occur around the time of menstruation and pregnancy respectively, yet there are many disagreements as to the actual time spans. Can PND be diagnosed one day, one week, one month, or one year after childbirth? If it can, does it remain the same 'depression', and can suggestions for a hormonal aetiology still be put forward? As with PMS, the lack of consistent evidence for psycho-biological influences in PND (Steiner 1979) challenges the assumptions of many researchers and practitioners. Similarly, the length of the premenstruation period as defined by different researchers and clinicians varies between one day to one week before menstruation, or, in some cases, the whole second half of the cycle. This makes a mockery of any comparison between studies, as very different experiences are being described under one umbrella term. I have argued that PMS is not a unitary phenomenon. The same has been said of PND (Hopkins *et al.* 1984), and with both 'disorders' the research data do not provide conclusive evidence for their existence. There is no clear theoretical framework within which to investigate PMS (Asso 1986) or PND (Nicolson 1988). As a result, a wide range of issues including aetiology, course, and treatment is investigated in an almost haphazard way. There is little interdisciplinary contact resulting in a split between the research which is attempting to find a biological explanation and that which is looking for psychological factors; few researchers attempt to incorporate both aspects of theory into their research. Nearly all researchers completely ignore the historical and political context within which these experiences are placed. This ignores a vital and important perspective for, as Ann Oakley said of postnatal depression, it 'is not a scientific term but an ideological one. It mystifies the real social and medical factors which lead to mothers' unhappiness' (Oakley 1979: 11–12). We could apply exactly the same analysis to PMS.

These broad definitions of 'disorders', which result in large proportions of women being labelled as suffering from PMS or PND, prevent us from offering appropriate help to those women who actually do suffer from medical disorders associated with menstruation or childbirth. The majority of women are experiencing unhappiness, anxiety and 'depression', not as a result of faulty hormonal systems but as a result of their oppression. Women's unhappiness is a reaction to the situations in which they find themselves. The labels which we put upon this unhappiness only serve to perpetuate the images of mad or bad women, adding to the contradictory discourses which surround womanhood.

Depression following childbirth is not confined to the immediate post-partum period. A large percentage of women with children under the age of five are diagnosed as depressed: Oakley (1986) reported that 42 per cent warrant the label of severe depression. It is not the biology of the women which is at fault, it is their experience of being a mother. In fact men who are the primary caregiver for young children have been shown to suffer more severely from depression than their female counterparts (Jenkins 1985). Although one must recognize that there are additional role and situational complications for men raising children, this is still evidence that the connection between depression and childrearing is social, not biological.

The alienation, and isolation, begin early in pregnancy and are reinforced by the experience of motherhood. The passive distress which women experience when they become mothers is only an intensification of what women are taught to feel about themselves as individuals from adolescence on.

Grieving the loss of self

A large contributory factor here is that, for many women, the reality of being pregnant, of pregnancy, and motherhood is so far from their prior ideal. Sheila Rossan (1987a) described how the first three months of motherhood were the most difficult, as women found it difficult to see themselves as 'good mothers'. Only through changing their self-attributions could they begin to make positive statements about themselves. As Paula Nicolson (1988) says, during pregnancy and following childbirth a woman '*needs* to go through a grieving process as a natural means of psychological reintegration which is not a sign of maladjustment or illness' (my emphasis).

As well as entailing the loss of the old self, pregnancy and motherhood cause changes in relationships with significant others: with a woman's partner (if she is in a stable relationship), with her friends, her mother and her work colleagues (Rossan 1987a). The changing relationship with a woman's mother may hinge on the fact that after the birth of the first child, the mother sees her daughter as an adult for the first time (Sayers 1988).

It is largely through these relational changes that major changes in identity are experienced. Thus pregnancy and childbirth need to be conceptualized as a complex interaction between the woman and her environment (Nicolson 1988). There is evidence to suggest that marital satisfaction decreases for many couples during pregnancy and following the birth of the first child (Feldman 1974; Rossan 1987a), with roles changing as many couples assume a more traditional pattern of behaviour in which the man has more power. For as Moss *et al.* (1987) note, in a study which reported that women carry out the majority of housework and childcare,

> There is no sign that the basic structure of the division of labour is being redesigned; having a baby confirms rather than challenges this structure. However, given women's increased participation and attainment in education and employment before having children, and some change in the climate of opinion about sex roles, the failure to produce a new structure may give rise increasingly to feelings of dissatisfaction and discontent, especially among women.
>
> (Moss *et al.* 1987: 85)

Whether this discontent is due to economic variables, power imbalances in the home, or the influence or the infantilization of women by the medical profession, the results are the same. The lack of power adds to the sense of alienation and loss of control which many women experience during the transition to motherhood, as motherhood 'subordinates women in almost all societies' (Nicolson 1988).

A large contributory factor in this subordination is that many women cease to hold positions of full-time employment after the second trimester of pregnancy, and thus become financially dependent on their partners or on the state. In addition, the loss of identity as an employee, with the concomitant loss of workmates, time structure and status, may result in the sense of isolation, lowering of self-esteem, and negative social and emotional effects which have been well documented in the unemployment literature (Jahoda 1982).

I'm mixed up really, because sometimes I want to be back at work. I really like the responsibility I had there. When I was at work, I had a very responsible job and people were demanding things here, there and everywhere. While I'm sitting here watching her playing on the floor, I think, well, I ought to be doing something with my mind. And the company — sometimes that's very bad. Sometimes I get really lonely, and when she's asleep I can't wait until she is back with me again. And when she's back, I think, well I wish I had somebody else I could talk to.

(Case study: Moss *et al*. 1986: 63)

Unemployment has a damaging effect on the marriage relationship and family life (Cochrane and Stopes-Roe 1981; Fagin 1981) and the loss of a job on either a temporary or a permanent basis during pregnancy or following childbirth may exacerbate difficulties in relationships and perhaps even produce them. It has also been suggested (Lewis 1987) that many women who would like to return to work following the birth of a child cannot do so because of the negative attitudes of employers who, despite the legislation to prevent this, replace women on maternity leave, or make it almost impossible for them to return to their original position, by enforcing an unacceptable drop in status. This results in a 'lack of congruence between the woman's intentions and wishes with regard to [employment] and their subsequent experiences as working mothers' (Lloyd 1987). Janice Long, whose radio show was chopped by the BBC after she gave birth, said: 'I don't know if you know this, but when you're a woman and you have a baby, your brain comes out with the afterbirth and you suddenly can't think' (*City Limits*, 5 May 1988: 4).

The exclusion of many women who become mothers from full-time employment, both through propaganda suggesting that 'a mother's place is in the home', and through the discriminatory political policies which limit childcare facilities, further acts to remove power and control from mothers: 'The dominant ideology about the role of the family and in particular about that of the mother, dictates an almost total lack of public respect and support for working parents and their children' (Lloyd 1987: 2). The statistical reality of this lack of respect is stark: of the 3 million children under five in Britain today, only 1 per cent are cared for in state nurseries. In this same group, 58 per cent of mothers have no regular support at all (Hunt 1987). Nine-tenths of European countries provide fathers with paternity leave which would give support: Britain doesn't allow one day.

The other side to this issue is that many women have no choice but to resume some sort of employment following childbirth because of economic necessity. Single mothers, as a group, are the poorest section of society, with the exception of pensioners. They have to rely on meagre state support for themselves and their children if they do not work outside the home. Yet as childcare facilities are limited and expensive, many women are caught in a poverty trap for which there is little relief. Many women who return to full-time work following the birth of their child experience strain between their role as a mother and their role as an employee. Anxiety and guilt often result because the socially-constructed ideal mother remains at home with her child. Lloyd (1987) describes a 'conflictual model' in describing the experience of mothers returning to full-time employment: a model which applies to women in both high and low status occupations. These women also viewed motherhood more negatively than women who remained at home with their child. However, these feelings related to 'the social context of motherhood, not to the child itself'. Thus it is not inevitable for women to experience alienation, powerlessness and role strain as a result of motherhood.

Women are faced with a double bind here as mothers. If they stay at home they are likely to be isolated and dependent, liable to suffer from alienation and depression. Conversely, if they go out to work, they invariably have to maintain a job, take the major role in childcare, and do the majority of the housework. Added to this is the guilt which many women experience in not being there for their children all the time. As Brigid McConville noted in a report of working mothers:

Pauline . . . worked nights, worked part-time, as a cleaner, a receptionist, a nurse, always having to fit her hours around the needs of her children. While at work she was always worried about the children: 'I had to leave before they went to school, so always I kept thinking: "Have they remembered the bus fare? Have they put warm clothes on?" and school holidays and weekends were always a problem. . . . I feel so bad about not being around all the time.'

(McConville 1987: 6)

This paradox, in which society decrees that motherhood is the crowning achievement of every woman's life yet women are prevented from taking part in many socially-valued activities (such as holding a full-time job) when they become mothers, leads to confusion and consternation for many women. This oppression is experienced as an assault on the self, as women feel devalued and restricted by both ideology and experience. Yet they are labelled depressed, as suffering from postnatal depression or the baby blues. It is the woman's 'raging hormones' at fault again and treatment is aimed at altering these. The social context is thus ignored and reinforced.

Sexuality and motherhood: the last taboo

The divisions of labour and allocations of power in patriarchy demand not merely a suffering mother, but one divested of sexuality: the Virgin Mary, virgo intacta, perfectly chaste. . . . If motherhood and sexuality were not wedged resolutely apart by male culture, if we could choose both the forms of our own sexuality and the terms of our motherhood or non-motherhood freely, women might achieve genuine sexual autonomy (as opposed to 'sexual liberation').

(Rich 1986: 184)

During pregnancy and motherhood one of the fundamental aspects of a woman's identity which is oppressed is sexuality. By defining women through the 'have/hold' discourse of sexuality (Hollway 1984) within the dichotomy of virgin/whore or mistress/mother, each woman is positioned. This defines sexuality as linked to reproduction, seeing women as both inherently asexual and possessed of a sexuality which is 'rabid and dangerous, and must be controlled' (Hollway 1984). This understanding of the discourse explains some of the confusion and contradictions regarding sexuality which women face when they become pregnant. The archetypal 'ideal' mother, the Madonna, who is asexual, pure, calm and tranquil, is at odds with the woman who has her own individual sexual identity. Defining sexuality as linked to reproduction, yet simultaneously denying the existence of sexuality in the pregnant woman or the mother, perpetuates the split between body and self which we first identified in the adolescent girl.

Researchers have traditionally emphasized this split between sex and motherhood, and only recently is it being investigated and challenged. Nadelson (1980) reported that many women experience great embarrassment over sexuality when they are pregnant, often seeing themselves as sacred or untouchable (Kitzinger 1983). This is a further example of how the influence of the madonna/whore dichotomy is perpetuated by women themselves through their 'interior colonization'. The internalization of the idea of asexual motherhood may explain the fact that a majority of women abstain from intercourse during pregnancy, without having been medically advised to do so (Solberg *et al.* 1973; Rossan 1987a). Thus it is almost inevitable that many women will suffer a major crisis in sexual identity at this time, as sexuality is inconsistent with their image of woman as mother. The medical profession perpetuates this, as many doctors are embarrassed to discuss sex with pregnant women, often not realizing that women have internalized the conflict. It has been suggested that many women seek consultations with their doctor during pregnancy with the express desire of discussing these issues and are put off by the doctor's perceived ambivalence (Reading 1983). If communication about sexual activity does take place between the doctor and the pregnant woman it tends to be advice to women perceived to be at risk of miscarriage to abstain from sexual intercourse in the first few months of pregnancy. Yet there is little evidence to suggest that intercourse and miscarriage are related, in the absence of other problems (Reading 1983; Kitzinger 1983). A worrying aspect of this practice is that many doctors do not tell women that it is all right to resume sexual activity after the first few months, when the suspected risk period is over. As a result, many couples abstain from any type of sexual activity for the whole pregnancy (Kitzinger 1983), assuming that a ban on intercourse means a ban on all sexual activity, which would not be the case.

The pervasiveness of the belief that sexual intercourse during pregnancy may harm the fetus causes this abstinence (Solberg *et al.* 1973). A further reason which has been postulated is physical discomfort. This could be alleviated by advice on the most suitable sexual positions for the pregnant woman, advice which can be found in many self-help books for women but which is rarely imparted by the medical profession. The anxiety and guilt which many women experience if they do have sex during pregnancy is potentially harmful for mother and child, further isolating the woman from both her identity as a sexual individual and her identity as a mother. This emphasis on intercourse, or genital acts, as the only means of expressing sexuality or experiencing sexual arousal reinforces the narrow definition of sexuality which restricts women in our society. If a wider definition of sexuality were used the potential discomfort of intercourse during the pre- or post-partum period would not be of such significance.

Sexuality and birth do not have to be exclusive experiences. Kitzinger (1983) has described how sex during pregnancy may have definite advantages for women: through reducing stress by causing the woman to feel loved and cherished, whilst the secretion of oxytocin, a hormone released during sexual arousal, acts to improve the tone of the contracting uterus. Psychoanalysts have equated giving birth with an almost painful sexuality, Deutch (1944) seeing the birth process as an 'orgy of masochistic pleasure'. Racamier (quoted by Nicolson 1988) believed that some women giving birth 'experience intense orgasmic pleasure', a finding reiterated by Kitzinger (1983) who describes the birth experience of some women as:

the most intensely sexual feeling a woman ever experiences, as strong as orgasm, even more compelling than orgasm. Some women find it disturbing because it is sexual and they feel out of control as the energy floods through them and they can do nothing to prevent it.

(Kitzinger 1983: 210)

So if sex, pregnancy and childbirth are related (and it has been argued that sex, labour and lactation are intrinsically interrelated (Newton 1973)), why do many women experience a split between their sexuality and their 'motherhood'? One reason is that 'sexual guilt and physical defilement in women are inextricably associated' throughout their pregnancy and childbirth (Rich 1986). Before the evolution of the science of motherhood, what maintained the split was the belief that the woman's body was evil:

There is a deep and prevalent sense of the woman's body as magical, as either vulnerable to or emanating evil — as unclean, and as the embodiment of guilt. These attitudes, internalised by her, affect her relationship to the birth process as much as do

ignorance, or the actual verifiable reality of risk and danger.
(Rich 1986: 164)

The other important factor is the attitude of the medical profession which treats pregnancy as an illness, in contrast to the woman-centred view that it is a life process. The different frames of reference adopted by the medical profession and by pregnant women, are rooted in the different social positions and perspectives of the two groups, and result in an exacerbation of the 'conflicting paradigms of pregnancy' (Graham and Oakley 1981). Inherent in the medicalization of pregnancy and childbirth, which has been well documented by Oakley (1975), is the removal of control from the woman and the depersonalization of the birth process, which infantilizes the woman. The use of high technology machinery, hospitalization, and the generally alienating nature of many women's experience of childbirth, strip all power from the woman, and further desexualize the experience. As Sheila Kitzinger has pointed out:

The intense sexuality of birth is in startling contrast to the institutional setting provided for the experience. It is as if we were required to make love . . . in a busy airport concourse, a large railway terminus, in a gymnasium, or a tiled public lavatory.
(Kitzinger 1983: 210)

There are slow changes happening in the medical profession, largely as a result of research documenting the alienated experiences of women under much of the present regime (Graham and Oakley 1981) combined with the increasingly vocal discontent of many women giving birth. One of the stronger movements in the last decade has been the change to methods of 'natural' childbirth. This has arisen directly as a result of the increasing use of medical technology in birth, which alienates women from the birth experience. However, one of the dangers in this is that one ideology is replaced with another: that women who have difficult births, or who suffer great pain and therefore request the intervention of the technology, are being unnatural. This is patently unrealistic. Pain is an intrinsic part of childbirth for the majority of women and removing the technology will not remove the pain, even if it does remove the alienation. The issue is not simply one of technological versus natural childbirth; it is not simply about the instruments used in birth, or the room in which it takes place. It is about a whole different approach to the pregnant woman: seeing childbirth in context, as part of the woman's whole life cycle; giving choice to the individual woman; treating her as a person and not removing control and power from her.

This is slowly happening. Under pressure, the medical profession is having to change. However, there is great reluctance to change on the part of many medical practitioners. This was evidenced by the treatment of the consultant obstetrician Wendy Savage in 1986, who was suspended from her post largely as a result of the opposition of her male colleagues to her advocacy of 'natural' methods of childbirth. Quite clearly the patriarchal medical profession is not easily going to relinquish the power which it enjoys at present in the realm of pregnancy and childbirth. Women must continue to fight to receive the service which is best for them. Birth plans and home births are means of reclaiming the territory of birth, reclaiming our bodies from the hands of the 'specialists'. This is one area in which psychology can work for women, for psychological research, which identifies the detrimental effect which a depersonalized birth process has on the individual woman, can be used to support the need for change in present practices. For example, one study (Sosa *et al*. 1980) reported that a group of women who received the support of one person throughout the whole birth process had a significantly shorter labour, fewer complications, and found the whole experience much more positive than a control group of women who did not receive the continuous support. This type of research can be used in the struggle towards a more woman-centred birth experience.

The issue of separation between sexuality and personal identity is an issue which continues after pregnancy and childbirth. Immediately following the birth women may feel separated from their bodies and find the thought of any sexual activity inconceivable. This will be exacerbated by maternity care which is clinical and alienating: for if a woman has been

processed through labour as if on a conveyer belt, with little or no choice about what happens to her, if she was probed and examined roughly and treated as the object of a medical exercise rather than as a person going through an experience of deep emotional significance, she is very likely to feel that her body no longer belongs to her but to the hospital, and later to find it very difficult to express herself through her body without inhibition.

(Kitzinger 1983: 218)

There is evidence that breastfeeding and nursing a child often cause highly charged sexual feelings (Rossi 1973), feelings which are denied by those who emphasize the importance of stimulating the child whilst ignoring a woman's sexual stimulation. Rossan (1987a) found that the sexual activities of a group of new mothers had declined markedly from their previous level; sensuous feelings, however, were being experienced during breastfeeding or whilst touching their baby's skin. The experience of sexual arousal during breastfeeding is a common one for many women, but will vary according to the same degree that breast sensitivity generally varies. To receive pleasure from nursing a child should be a positive aspect of female experience, but because of the split between sex and motherhood, many women cannot cope with this experience.

there are strong cultural forces which desexualise women as mothers, the orgasmic sensations felt in childbirth or while suckling infants have probably until recently been denied even by the women feeling them, or have evoked feelings of guilt. Yet, as Newton reminds us, 'Women . . . have a more varied heritage of sexual enjoyment than men'.

(Rich 1986: 183)

In fact it has been suggested (Pryor 1973) that many women completely refuse to breastfeed because of fears of sexual arousal, which causes feelings of guilt, shame and fears of sexual perversion.

The mindless perpetuation of this split fragments a woman's identity. To be a mother by choice as well as a sexual person should be every woman's right. If parenting, rather than mothering, were practised, rather than talked about, by a large number of adults, neither scholars nor mothers would have such a problem with maternal sexuality.

Body image: changing size, changing self

In our examination of the development of personal identity in the adolescent in Chapter 2 we examined the importance of body image and changing body size on a woman's concept of self. During pregnancy there are dramatic changes in body shape and size, changes which many women feel extremely ambivalent about:

> I was both fascinated and horrified by my body when pregnant. I thought it beautiful, that mound of glistening flesh, but also obscene — a tumour of some kind. Indeed, one had no control over its growth. And one's breasts grew too, heavy, changing their angles, striped with blue veins, ready to be, it seemed, the world's dairy.
>
> (Oakley 1986: 59)

The changes in a woman's body which take place during pregnancy have a considerable effect on personal identity and image of self. As we have discussed in relation to adolescence, women are defined by their bodies; their bodies are expected to buy them happiness. In our society, where women are expected to have slim (and, today, fit) young bodies, it is almost only during pregnancy that it is socially acceptable to be large. Some women find their new freedom to eat a positive benefit of pregnancy:

> I must admit, I do enjoy being able to eat three meals a day, saying it's for the baby, and not having to worry about whether I'll get into my clothes again, or whether my stomach is bulging. I'll worry about losing the weight afterwards!
>
> (Helen, 5 months pregnant)

However, there are other women who view their new larger bodies with fear and disgust, and experience some of the feelings of loss of control suffered by adolescents:

> I couldn't wait to have the baby: I felt so disgusted with my figure — all that dieting gone down the drain. I felt as if people were staring at me all of the time — thinking how disgusting I looked: like a large beached whale.
>
> (Eileen)

The same mechanisms, by which changes in body size and shape affect identity throughout the life cycle, exert their influence on the pregnant woman. With the growth of the child the abdomen will grow and the genitals will change in texture and colour, the labia becoming engorged like that of a sexually aroused woman. Depending on their attitude to these changes, women will look on their changing bodies with enjoyment and delight, marvelling at their growth, or view themselves with horror. In the latter case the woman experiences further alienation from her self. The contradictory discourses which say 'attractive woman = slim' and 'woman = mother' mean that a woman cannot be attractive and be pregnant, or a new mother, at the same time.

Research carried out with anorexic women who become pregnant (Stewart *et al.* 1987) showed that their illness went into remission for the duration of the pregnancy, and there seemed to be fairly good adjustment to the changing size. No doubt this is because it is only during pregnancy that women in present day Western society can be large, look fat, and be proud of themselves.

Childlessness: the curse of the barren womb

> The womb
> Rattles its pod, the moon
> Discharges itself from the tree with nowhere to go.
>
> My landscape is a hand with no lines,
> The roads bunched to a knot,
> The knot myself,
>
> Myself the rose you achieve —
> This body
> This ivory
>
> Ungodly as a child's shriek.
> Spiderlike I spin mirrors,
> Loyal to my image,
>
> Uttering nothing but blood —
> Taste it, dark red!
> And my forest
>
> My funeral,
> And this hill and this
> Gleaming with the mouths of corpses.
>
> (Plath, 1962)

In a world where womanhood is synonymous with motherhood, the situation of women who remain childless is an interesting one. Some remain childless through choice, whilst a more despairing group of women want children but find themselves unable to do so.

Infertility has been estimated to affect 16 per cent of couples in Britain (Hull *et al.* 1985). It has been suggested that psychological difficulties such as depression or anxiety, as well as marital problems, may occur as a result of this childlessness (Mahlstedt 1985), with women generally being more adversely affected than men (Raval *et al.* 1987). In a recent study it was estimated that a significant percentage of infertile couples would welcome more psychological support than that which was then on offer (Edelmann and Connolly 1987), which suggests that the effects of childlessness cannot be easily dismissed.

Childless women are a devalued group in society, seen as unnatural and unfulfilled: in failing to become mothers they fail to become women (Woollett 1987). Women who elect to remain childless are seen as mad, deviant, or pitiful, as Greene (1963) in an article 'I don't want to be a mother' illustrated: 'stating such a preference was met with as much shock as if she had announced she was running for the Communist Party cell block in her basement!' (p. 10). Society pities those women who are childless against their wishes and the pity reinforces their sense of worthlessness. The language which positions these women within the discourses of woman and mother is negative and degrading: barren, unfruitful, addle, arid — they all mean 'of no effect', or unproductive. If women are expected to receive their status and identity through childrearing, what is the fate of childless women? As this woman who had no children remarked: 'It is possible to survive, but never to recover from the knowledge that one has failed to fulfil the basic requirement of all living creatures — to reproduce. . . . The failure one feels is grinding' (NHR Newsletter 38, quoted in McConville 1987: 22).

The construction of their childlessness as failure allows us to see the powerful way in which women are defined by their reproductive capabilities. One of the crises which occurs for women who choose to pursue a career is the realization in their thirties that it is 'now or never'. The feeling that the 'reproductive' clock is rapidly ticking away affects many women in this group unnecessarily. It is a complicated double bind at present, for, as Adrianne Rich notes, 'Mothering and non-mothering have been such highly charged concepts for us, precisely because whichever we did has been turned against us' (Rich 1986: 253).

Women in a paradox

There is an assumption that the archetypal feminine personality is one which is 'right' for mothering. However, as Breen (1975) reported that traditionally feminine women had the most problems coping with pregnancy, this assumption is erroneous. The passivity of femininity contrasts sharply with the strength and perseverance necessary for mothering, leaving women in a paradox. Many women, besides those who do not exhibit 'feminine characteristics' or who express discontent, don't fit into our present archetype of motherhood. For example, women with learning difficulties or a mental handicap are often denied the choice of being a mother, being seen as children themselves (Roberts and Burns 1987). The recent court case of 'Jeanette', in which a young woman with learning difficulties was forcibly sterilized, highlights the extremes to which society will go to prevent certain women who are deemed unfit from having access to motherhood.

Women who have chosen a lesbian way of life are seen as deviant, and frequently encounter more than passive resistance in their efforts to become mothers. There is no evidence that children socialized in a lesbian relationship suffer from any ill effects (Green 1978) as those who condemn the homosexual community would have us believe, yet the ideological framework which surrounds female homosexuality is opposed to the possibility of motherhood on these grounds. Similarly, women who have children outside marriage have traditionally been considered deviant by society.

A dismantling of the ideology of pregnancy and motherhood will involve challenging many of the present contradictory discourses through which women are constructed as passive reproducers, ideal mothers, or, more frequently, failures. We need to construct our own discourses, which will define success in terms which are appropriate for each woman and her particular context. Women already evaluate success in pregnancy and childbirth differently from the medical profession (Graham and Oakley 1981), which generally represents the dominant ideology in our society. If a woman at the moment

> feels in any way discordant with the mothering role as she has constructed it (or the one constructed by her particular context) [she] will assess herself as 'poorly adjusted' or 'ill' because that is

how she can best fit to her view of the rest of society.

(Nicolson 1986: 135)

The way forward would seem to be to construct our own discourses about mothering, which will allow these experiences to be viewed positively and realistically. Women's experiences of unhappiness should be validated as a normal and natural reaction to changes in self and identity, or a reaction to a restricted life, not invalidated through being understood as an illness. If this makes women aware of their oppression as mothers, surely it is better to equip them to be more assertive and to control their own destinies than to dismiss their justifiable anguish as 'postnatal depression', an internal pathological syndrome. It is perhaps an inevitable aspect of becoming a mother for many women that the change in identity, loss of the old self, will result in sadness.

Accompanied by the physical complications and the practical realities of motherhood, one might expect all women to experience distress and discomfort. We need to reconstruct our images of mothers to incorporate the reality rather than the fantasy, thereby allowing women to experience unhappiness without perceiving themselves to be failures. At the same time we cannot ignore the fact that for many women in our society motherhood is an alienating and isolating experience. Lack of child support, isolation in the home and economic dependence on others will have dramatic effects on a woman's self-concept, and weaken her self identity. Through applying an analysis, in which a woman is always seen in the context of her own life and birth and pregnancy are seen as part of the life cycle, we can move towards understanding the true cause of unhappiness during pregnancy and following childbirth in the individual woman, and attempt to provide more effective methods of intervention. We can also offer alternative ways of viewing pregnancy and motherhood: ways which are more positive and forward reaching, regarding both as part of the life cycle and — although important to the individual woman — no more important than the woman herself. As Stephanie Dowrick proclaimed:

I believe it can be different. We are truly victims if we cannot create those new realities. We are undone unless we break those rules which can and do make of motherhood a prison and a burden. I would be undone if I had to forsake the rest of my life as a price for motherhood. The twigs of a nest would soon rub me raw. I want to expand my limits by having a child, not reduce my world, no matter how precious my fellow occupant.

(Dowrick 1980: 71)

Chapter 5

Menopause: a time of change

> The death of the reproductive faculty (during the menopause) is accompanied . . . by struggles which implicate every organ and every function of the body.
>
> (Smith 1848: 607)

> The . . . 'change of life', as it is commonly called, frequently leads to periods of insanity . . . because certain functions then cease, and the constitution is thereby always more or less deranged.
>
> (Morrison 1848: 292)

The discourse which traditionally locates female 'insanity' (within the scientific paradigm now relabelled 'symptoms' or 'syndromes') in the female body defines the menstruating woman and the postmenopausal woman as dangerously subject to her reproductive organs. Just as menstruation is used to dismiss and control behaviour through the perpetuation of a negative and damaging ideology, so is the menopause.

The discourse which defines women through their reproductive function conceptualizes the biological event of menopause as the end of a woman's useful life. As fertility and femininity are immutably linked here, women who lose their fertility often experience the simultaneous loss of their femininity, a major part of their identity as a woman. Within this discourse, sexuality is inseparable from reproduction, so that the postmenopausal woman is defined as asexual and redundant. 'Women are permitted to be sexual only at a certain time of life, and the sensuality of mature — and certainly of aging — women has been perceived as grotesque, threatening, and inappropriate' (Rich 1986: 183).

Dickson (1986) has claimed that a woman's sexuality is her main resource in the present economic system. At menopause, society strips women of their sexuality, and thus, if one follows Dickson's argument, strips women of their main resource.

> What, fat, forty-three, and I dare to think I'm still a person? No, I am an invisible lump. I belong to a category labelled a priori without interest to anyone . . . the mass media tell us all day, all evening long that we are inadequate, mindless, ugly, disgusting in ourselves. . . . Think what it is like to have most of your life ahead of you and be told you are obsolete. Think what it is like to feel attraction, desire, affection towards others . . . and to be told every day that you are not a woman but a tired object that should disappear.
>
> (Moss (1970) quoted by Itzen 1986: 129)

Is this the fate of all women: to feel obsolete at forty-three, to feel invisible and inadequate? Are the last forty years of a woman's life inevitably spent looking back in longing at the years of youth and fertility? No. This negative construing is not an inevitable process: the horrors of the menopause are not experienced by all women. In fact there is evidence to suggest that expectations of the worst are rarely fulfilled, and many women do find a new lease of life after the menopause. A new generation of women, influenced by the feminist reconceptualization of the female role, are reaching middle age without a concomitant sense of redundancy, as they have active, fulfilling lives not centred on their reproductive powers. Yet anxieties about uselessness, asexuality and lack of identity are real for many women during the menopause. We will see that the anxieties are invariably not the result of internal hormonal changes, as many experts might suggest, but of a complex interrelationship between psychological and social factors involving the internalization of a set of negative constructs which reproduce society's view of the menopausal woman.

The menopause, then, is another stage in the life cycle in which a woman's reproductive cycle is used to account for and dismiss her behaviour. It is used to condemn her to a limited role and is blamed for any problems or complaints which ensue. Once again biological determinism avoids any analysis of the social or political context in which women exist.

Menopausal changes are only a part of the continuum of our lives: they do not occur in isolation. The menstrual taboo exerts its influence on women's lives, framing their experiences from the onset of menarche to the final menstrual flow. This taboo is lifted at menopause, but a whole set of other taboos and restrictions contained within the discourse of woman as reproductive vessel ensures the ideology of reproduction maintains its control of women's lives.

Menopause, climacteric, the change: a matter of semantics?

A distinction is increasingly being made between the menopause — the biological event of the cessation of menstruation with the concomitant hormonal changes — and the climacteric, the whole phase of life from 45–65 years of age during which women pass from 'middle age' to 'old age'. During this period menstrual cycle changes are only part of the changes taking place. Climacteric changes occur in both men and women: the classic 'mid-life crisis' is becoming an accepted clinical entity as well as being the stuff of much popular mythology. During the fourth and fifth decade of life, both men and women find themselves reassessing past goals and ambitions, examining the future with a mixture of anticipation and dread. It is not inevitable that this process is a crisis. However, the menopause as a biological transition, due to hormonal changes which occur as ovulation ceases, is peculiar to women. In addition, this mid-life period is conceptualized very differently for men and women, the associations attached to women's ageing being much more negative than those attached to men's.

The 'menopause' tends to be blamed for any problems and all of the changes (both physical and psychological) which take place during the later stages of a woman's life. It has been said that in their thirties women are seen as 'pre-menopausal', in their forties 'menopausal', and in their fifties 'post-menopausal' (Levine and Doherty 1952). Women themselves are encouraged to use this method of categorization, to such an extent that, in her research on the menopause, Fiona Goudie (1986) could report one of her respondents saying: '[I have been] suffering with this menopause for twenty years (since the age of twenty-five) and it started my mental breakdown' (Goudie 1986: 83).

The fact that the differentiation between the climacteric and the menopause is a distinction which many practitioners, researchers, and women themselves do not make, in itself leads to many problems. There are problems of definition in particular which may be part of the same euphemistic process which I have discussed in relation to PMS (see pp. 45–8). The term 'menopause' is most commonly used by women themselves (as well as many professionals) for *all* of the changes which take place during this period of life. The *Oxford English Dictionary* informs us that 'meno-' is a derivation from the Greek, meaning month. 'Menopause' means a monthly cessation. However, there is a cessation of more than the monthly blood-loss of menstruation during this phase of a woman's life. There is the cessation of the influence of the menstrual taboo; the cessation of the ability to bear children and of the possibility of being confined by that ability: there is the cessation of the tendency to be defined solely through reproduction. One could argue that there is a cessation of many other aspects of a woman's identity at this point in the life cycle, which are bound up with being fertile, capable of mothering, and being a 'young' woman. These changes in identity can be conceptualized as either positive or negative, depending on the individual woman and the degree to which she has internalized the ideology of the redundant menopausal woman.

'Climacteric', the preferred term for a growing number of 'experts', is defined as 'constituting a crisis, critical (physiological and medical), occurring at the period of life (45–60) at which vital force begins to decline' (*OED*, 1970 edition). The assumptions contained within this term are antipathetic to a feminist analysis of the mid-life experiences of women, as they infer both crisis and loss of vitality. Neither of these necessarily, or inevitably, occurs.

Neurgarten and Kraines (1965) distinguish between the menopause, which is a 'discrete physiological event marked by the cessation of menstruation', and the climacteric, 'a long term physiological process, caused by the involution of the ovaries' (Cooke 1984). There would seem to be little distinction between these definitions. Both are locating problems within the woman herself, in her reproductive organs, and are thus misleading.

The menopause is an 'archetypal female experience' (Lennert and Willson 1973), a distinct phase of life, a *rite de passage* as important as menarche, and needs to be clearly distinguishable from the male 'climacteric'. Women themselves generally refer to

107

this whole phase of life as the 'menopause'. To change the terminology under the guise of being more specific and accurate only serves to isolate women from their experience, convincing them that 'doctor knows best', and reinforcing the influence of the scientific rhetoric which perpetuates the mythology of the expert. For this reason, I will use the term 'menopause' to refer to the whole mid-life phase of a woman's life, generally recognized as being from approximately forty-five to sixty years of age (obviously with individual variations). Many changes takes place during this period, of which the cessation of menstruation is but one. Cessation and change in other areas of life are of equal importance, and may be said to be of much greater significance to women than the absence of the monthly blood-loss. I feel that it is important to use a term which distinguishes between those mid-life changes experienced by men and women. They are intrinsically different, both because of the biological changes unique to women and the differences in the social constructions of this period of life for men and women.

Careful attention to language and terminology is important for other reasons besides. In Chapter 2, I argued that the language used to describe the female genitals and the experience of menstruation was both derogatory and negative: the implications of this were seen to be in damage to women's conceptualizations of self, with repercussions in experiences of 'problems' and 'syndromes'. This same negative language is used to describe the menopause, and the changes which take place during this phase of the life cycle:

> the way in which the menopause has been written about by predominately male doctors who describe 'vaginal atrophy', 'degenerative changes', 'oestrogen starvation' and 'senile pelvic involution' conditions women to see each sign of the menopause as a stigma by which they are labelled as aging and 'past it'.
>
> (Kitzinger 1983: 237)

This is in sharp contrast to the language used to describe changes which men experience at this phase of the life cycle, and parallels the gender difference we observed in the earlier chapter in descriptions of male genitalia.

> We do not have 'testicular insufficiency' to match 'ovarian insufficiency' or 'senile scrotum' to match 'senile ovaries'. In the *Merck Manual of Diagnosis and Therapy*, the common

physicians' handbook, in describing premature menopause, specific medical directions are given for 'preservation of a serviceable vagina'. Do you think there is equal discussion of a 'serviceable penis'?. . . . Of course there isn't. When a doctor injects testosterone in a man, it is not for the purpose of preserving or creating a 'serviceable penis' . . . men do not serve. Women do. The purpose is to increase his libido, to raise his hormone level.

(Reitz 1981: 73)

Menopause or mid-life crisis: lifting the menstrual curse

In popular consciousness, the changes taking place during the menopause are *all* negative, inevitable, and debilitating. Many women dread its approach:

I look at every new wrinkle, every grey hair and think of the time when I won't be able to cope with anything: when I'll probably finally go mad. Isn't it true that women who are going through the change are out of their minds for most of the time?

(Melanie, aged 30)

I'd like to know what to expect from the menopause. I tend to be nervous and edgy now . . . I worry about going crazy or losing all control when I reach menopause. I'm twenty-one now, so I'll just have to wait and see.

(D. G., quoted by Weideger 1982: 206)

The interpretation of why some women are affected to a greater degree than others differs according to the aetiological stance one takes. By far the most ubiquitous is the medical one which, as we have seen in relation to the menstrual cycle and pregnancy, adopts a pathological model in order to interpret a wide range of different experiences. We need to examine how this approach has been used to categorize, then treat, women with a wide range of menopausal problems, before we can finally argue for a reconceptualization of our minds and bodies, throwing off the cloak of 'illness'.

The return of the raging hormones: medicalization missing the boat again

As is the case with PMS and PND, conceptualizing menopausal

women within a disease model attributes problems to internal, biological factors, and then treats them accordingly. Early medical interventions for female 'insanity' occurring in menopausal women were extreme, brutal and undeniably misogynist, including courses of injections of water into the rectum and the application of leeches to the labia (see p. 7).

The medical profession no longer uses clitoridectomy or leeching to deal with menopausal insanity, but one might argue that they are using the same ideological framework as did their forebears to judge what is normal and what is 'insane'. And it is their definitions which help produce that insanity. They stimulate the fear with which many women approach middle age: the stereotype of the asexual, incompetent, depressed, and ridiculous older woman is both pervasive and powerful. 'No woman can be sure of escaping the horror of this living decay. Every woman faces the threat of extreme suffering and incapacity' (R. A. Wilson 1966: a major proponent of HRT, writing on the menopause, quoted in Goudie 1986: 85).

In recent years this 'insanity', or 'living decay', is seen as being manifested in a wide but vague array of psychological and physical symptoms. What exactly are these problems which women experience, and how debilitating are they? In a review of five surveys, Greene (1984) reported that the most common physical symptoms experienced by women during the menopause are hot flushes (experienced by 68 per cent of women), dizzy spells (32 per cent), rheumatic pains (32 per cent), and a dryness of the vaginal walls, reported by a large number of women. It is the reduction of oestrogen as a result of ovarian involution which is the cause of this vaginal dryness. The cervix and the uterus may shrink, leading to general pelvic involution and a tendency to incontinence (Lauritzen and Muller 1977). It has also been suggested that metabolic changes take place as a result of the withdrawal of oestrogen. A loss of calcium in the bone, osteoporosis, may result in a higher incidence of hip or spinal fractures (Prill 1978), apparently six to ten times greater than men of the same age group.

There is a lack of agreement as to the specific psychological symptoms associated with the menopause. Greene (1984) reported that the most common were depression (49 per cent), which was described as feeling unhappy, and irritability (64 per cent), which was described as feeling 'wound up'. Other studies describe headaches, nervousness, feelings of suffocation, palpitations, sleeplessness, and weight gain. As Hunter *et al.* (1986) note, the lack of clear guidelines as to the epidemiological status of the menopausal complaints results in inconsistencies in diagnosis and disagreement as to whether particular symptoms are due to the menopause or to social factors. The lack of agreement associated with the specific symptoms attributable to the menopause is reminiscent of the lack of specificity associated with the symptoms of the premenstrual syndrome and postnatal depression. In fact many of the 'menopausal' symptoms are the same as those supposedly part of PMS, further reinforcing our argument that PMS is not a discrete syndrome. It has been argued by other researchers that the symptoms found in menopausal women are not peculiar to this phase of life, as they may be experienced at any time during the life cycle (Brown and Brown 1976).

In an attempt to provide some clarity, Greene (1984) grouped the wide range of symptoms into psychological, somatic (i.e., dizziness), and vasomotor (i.e., hot flushes), as a means of distinguishing possible aetiological factors. It has been suggested (Cooke 1980) that it is only the vasomotor symptoms which significantly increase during or following the biological events of the menopause, which suggests that it is only these symptoms which may have some aetiological base in the hormonal changes.

Although a large number of women report that they experience some noticeable physical or psychological problems during the menopause, it is estimated that only 10 per cent of women are debilitated in any way by them. However, if one in ten women are seriously affected this is clearly an issue which needs to be investigated. These symptoms are generally 'treated' by means of hormone replacement therapy (HRT), based on the premise that the menopause is a 'deficiency disease'. It is the absence of oestrogen which is considered to be at the root of the wide range of symptoms. Once ovarian function ceases, as is the case during the menopause, oestrogen levels do fall considerably. Yet this is not a sudden decline, as oestrogen levels fall gradually from the midtwenties onwards (Kitzinger 1983), so why is falling oestrogen not implicated in all of the problems which women experience from their twenties onwards? Perhaps because it is not at the root of the problem.

HRT is seen as a panacea by many of the practitioners who deal with menopausal women and their problems. Wilson warned that 'without HRT [women] would become like eunuchs and be crippled by what was happening to them' (Kitzinger 1983). Yet there is little evidence for the efficacy of HRT in curing the wide range of reported menopausal problems. In a review of ten controlled clinical trials, hot flushes and vaginal dryness were the only symptoms which were reduced following HRT (Greene 1984). In addition, in three of these trials it was reported that a placebo was as effective as HRT in reducing *all* symptoms. None of the psychological symptoms experienced by women, such as depression, anxiety, or irritability, were in any way relieved by HRT.

It has been suggested (Goudie 1986) that the vasomotor symptoms of hot flushes and the vascular symptoms of vaginal dryness are the only menopausal symptoms which have an aetiological base in the hormonal changes, which is why they may be alleviated by HRT. Yet any middle-aged woman who attends her local doctor's surgery complaining of tiredness, lack of enthusiasm for life, depression, etc., will most probably be given HRT as a 'cure', on the assumption that all problems are caused by deficient oestrogen; the hormones are raging again. Women themselves will often ask for HRT out of a sense of desperation, as well as lack of information about alternatives. Many seem to be expecting miracles: one could suggest that they are wanting their life situation to change, not just their own 'symptoms':

I decided to have HRT because arguments with my husband were becoming more exaggerated. I've always been argumentative but things are worse now. I had to have HRT to see if the arguments were due to me and my hormones or him. Maybe he's going through the change! If HRT helps the arguments I'll know it's me.

(Case study: Goudie 1986: 59)

One could argue that many of the women who ask for HRT when they go to their local doctor complaining of menopausal symptoms are victims of advertising and the self-help books which advocate replacement of a woman's deficient hormones as the only available intervention. This is not to deny that some women do experience symptom relief following HRT, either genuine or the placebo effect, as one woman reported:

I started on Cyclo-Progynova and it changed my life. I get no side-effects at all. At the Older Feminists there seemed to be an incredible amount of fear and prejudice about HRT. This is my experience — I have been taking it for more than two years and haven't regretted it for a second. You women who light up your twentieth cigarette of the day and tell me I'll get cancer — give up the fags and improve your life with HRT!

(Case study: Kitzinger 1983: 236)

Women are encouraged to seek local relief for vaginal dryness through the use of oestrogen creams which are absorbed into the vaginal walls. However, as it has been suggested that long-term use of exogenous oestrogen could lead to a high risk of endometrial cancer (Nathenson and Lorenz 1982), this practice may be dangerous. There are alternatives to oestrogen for, as Kitzinger (1983) suggests, a simple lubricant cream to ease any sexual activity can be as effective. A recent report of the World Health Organization (1981) has challenged the use of oestrogen in treating menopausal symptoms, stating that in '70–80 per cent of post-menopausal women the level of circulating oestrogen is sufficient'. As it has also been suggested that HRT is significantly correlated with cancer of the breast and uterus as well as clotting disorders, the ease with which many women are prescribed this treatment is alarming.

Despite all of this information, the majority of doctors are still more likely to prescribe hormones to menopausal women than to consider any other form of advice, support, or intervention. The number of prescriptions of oestrogen has been shown to have tripled between 1971 and 1977 to 1.2 million women per year (Anderson and McPherson 1984). In the USA a survey showed that 51 per cent of menopausal women received HRT for a minimum of three months, with the median time for treatment being 10 years (Stadel and Weiss 1975). Recent literature for GPs maintains that 'it is lack of oestrogen that causes the majority of symptoms and pathology of the menopause' (Paterson 1985). Thus it would seem that the attribution of women's experiences and symptoms to our 'raging hormones' is not on the decline.

A second 'cure' for gynaecological problems during the meno-pausal years is hysterectomy, an operation involving removal of the uterus, the bleeding womb which is believed to be at the root of all problems. It is an operation which is carried out on the basis of a

113

woman's subjective assessment of her problems (Kincey and McFarlane 1984), rather than because of an objective need for the surgery, and is thus often based on judgements of heavy bleeding or dysmenorrhea. In one study it was reported that 52 per cent of women underwent hysterectomy because of heavy bleeding (Hodges 1987). As it was shown that women use very different subjective criteria when deciding whether or not their menstrual bleeding is heavy (with some women who lose very small quantities of blood defining it as heavy, and vice-versa), it seems dangerous to carry out major surgery as a result of these beliefs. Hysterectomy is an operation whose efficiacy has never been accurately assessed. It is assumed to cure all problems, which it undoubtedly does not, and it can in fact often result in severe psychological problems for the individual woman. The ease with which the medical profession removes the womb is more of a reflection of misogynist attitudes towards the female body and reproduction than a reflection of the need for the operation.

What is vital is that alternative therapies are developed for the group of women who experience physical discomfort during the menopause. One suggestion is relaxation therapy (Notman and Nadelson 1979) which has been shown to be effective with menstrual-cycle symptomatology. Self-help groups which act to raise women's consciousness about the roots of their experiences may also be of benefit, reducing isolation whilst providing a forum within which women can reframe their lives in a way which is both positive and meaningful for each individual. A further suggestion is the use of cognitive restructuring techniques: relabelling symptoms as less negative, or altering one's attributions concerning the aetiology of symptoms. An example of this relabelling is provided by Sheila Kitzinger, who suggests that hot flushes need not be the negative experience one might expect:

a hot flush can look very attractive. . . . I liked the rosy glow. From that moment on I decided that hot flushes were life-enhancing. Once you can think positively about a hot flush, the sensations experienced may change their quality too. Each flush is wave-like, rather like a contraction in labour, or like a wave of sexual feeling sweeping through the body. It is possible to go with it rather than against it or trying to pretend it is not happening.
(Kitzinger 1983: 234)

Thus a change in the cognitive labels which one attaches to symptoms may alter the experience to make it less negative. This is akin to the arousability hypothesis in the menstrual cycle, derived from the work of Schacter and Singer (1962) discussed in Chapter 3.

The second cognitive strategy would be to examine the attributions which women make for menopausal symptoms, and work on these to allow alternative coping skills to develop. This attributional process is the same as that which we have observed with the menstrual cycle, in which women attributed negative symptoms to their cycle and positive symptoms to their environment. It was suggested that by manipulating these attributions, women could look for alternative causative explanations, and thus relabel the 'symptoms' within their own framework (Koeske 1977). It has been shown that women use this same process with menopausal symptoms, attributing negative moods to the menopause, whereas positive moods are attributed to personality or the situation (Perlmutter and Bart 1982).

There is no direct evidence for a relationship between hormonal changes taking place during the menopause and psychological symptoms experienced. Hormonal interventions do not necessarily alleviate psychological symptoms, and women who report emotional or psychological problems have not been shown to be deficient in oestrogen. It is obviously erroneous, therefore, to attribute any psychological symptoms to the biological changes which are taking place: 'menopausal emotionality' as a biological weakness is a myth. It is not our internal chemistry which we should be examining in order to provide an explanation for psychological problems experienced during the menopausal years. Instead, we should look to the meaning of menopause in society, and to the socio-cultural changes which are taking place for women during these years.

Limited roles: limited lives?

There is a veil of mystery surrounding this natural womanly function. At worst it is labelled a disease and shrouded in fear. At best menopause has become a catch-all for all the physical and emotional problems of women between the ages of forty and fifty-five.

(Golden 1984: 74)

The attribution of any negative psychological symptoms experienced in the middle years of a woman's life to a biologically determined syndrome, the menopause, is largely possible because of the negative attitudes which society holds towards women in this stage of their lives. This is not surprising, given the limited social roles open to women and the general conceptualization of the post-menopausal woman as barren and useless.

In modern Western society, the processes of ageism and sexism combined to define women as useless when they reach the end of their reproductive years: condemning them to 30 years of half-life. Alex Comfort (1977) has distinguished between biological and sociogenic ageing, identifying the 'arbitrary rolelessness of retirement' as a primary factor in the experience of uselessness which determines 'sociogenic' ageing. However, we must acknowledge the gender differential in this ageing process. The 'arbitrary rolelessness' is experienced by many women long before the official age for retirement from paid work (60−65 years of age at present in Britain). As we have previously discussed, women are encouraged to seek their identity and self-definition in society through their capacity to reproduce. Planning a family, having children, and caring for them, provide employment and a meaningful role. The loss of this role, without the substitution of another, may accelerate the process of sociogenic ageing.

This advent of ageing is experienced as a crisis by many women: a crisis which is not experienced in the same way by men. Within the discourses concerning women, looking young is seen to be one of our main preoccupations: our images of 'ideal women', against whom all women are judged and against which we as women judge ourselves, are primarily of young, slim, able-bodied, heterosexual, attractive women. The media, acting as an 'agent of socialisation' (Ferguson 1983), blast out these images at us from every advertising hoarding, every magazine cover, and every television and cinema screen. Women's magazines are 'formative in actually shaping women's experiences' (Winship 1983), through providing mirror images for our judgement, the 'media woman' against whom all women are compared. Older women are mostly absent from these images: if present, they are largely represented as an incapable, unattractive group.

When older women are portrayed — on the few occasions when

they are not invisible by complete omission — they are exorted to stay young and beautiful, to do things to their bodies to achieve this, and to wear make-up, hair products and clothes to conceal their real age. They, more often than men, are shown as weak and helpless . . . categorized by exclusion in relation to romance, sex and leisure . . . in dependent roles — as pensioners in clubs or dependent on a man. Or they are shown as victims of violent muggings, especially of 'Granny-bashing'.

(Itzen 1986: 126)

This analysis of the type of representation which exists is important to us, as it highlights the powerful influence which media images have in the formation of a woman's identity, and in shaping women's experiences. If women are only represented as either attractive, sexual, and young, or unattractive, older, and boring/bored, it is not surprising that these later years are approached with dread.

Media images of women, reflecting society's construction of the narrow female role, depict childbearers and childrearers. If we look at the 'media woman', her main concern from adolescence onwards is to 'catch' a man. She makes herself as attractive as possible so as to achieve this aim. When she achieves it and becomes a wife and mother, she is shown to be solely interested in keeping her family to the best of her ability. Marjorie Ferguson carried out a content analysis of three women's magazines during the years 1949–74 and 1979–80, and found that 67 per cent of the themes were of women in this latter role.

Once she has caught her man, the 'media woman' occupies herself with finding the best washing powder, or fabric softener, so as to please her family, apparently obtaining a great deal of satisfaction from such tasks. Her house is spotless, her children smiling, and she looks as if she were having the time of her life. The real-life woman can never be as perfect as the media woman: her family and home will never be as well run, and she may even find that there is little satisfaction in the role she has been building up to for years. Yet these images are doubly inaccurate, as most women no longer live in the traditional, purely domestic, manner depicted. Women comprise 40 per cent of the workforce, with 60–73 per cent of married women working outside the home. In Ferguson's study only 7 per cent of themes related to women as having careers. This role is not a salient part of the discourse which frames and confines women, and thus is underemphasized. As we saw in Chapter 1 (p. 15) the career woman is painted as dangerous and threatening, if she is shown at all. Yet working women still do the majority of the domestic work in the home (Kenny 1983), an imbalance which is undoubtedly reinforced by the prevalence of the 'media woman', the super-mum who manages to cope with everything.

There is no positive role for women in the media once they have had their children, and their looks are fading. Women from their mid-forties onwards have low status and little value, in contrast to men of the same age group who are told that they are in the prime of their lives and who often experience a continuing increase in status and value as their careers progress.

Women are exhorted to use magical creams to erase the lines of age, to wear restrictive corsets to hide the unattractive bulging flesh and, if all else fails, to submit to cosmetic surgery to rejuvenate their looks and return to a more youthful appearance. Whilst a fifty-year-old man is seen as distinguished and attractive, his age almost enhancing his sexuality, a fifty-year-old woman is seen as embarrassing if she intimates that she is sexually active. There are few female role models to suggest that a woman can still be sexually attractive after the 'first flush of youth' has passed. Those who do exist — for example, Joan Collins, the *Dynasty* soap-opera star — are seen as exceptions, rather than as representative of their age group or as real women. The media interest in Joan Collins, and others like her, is mainly centred on the seemingly amazing fact that she is still sexually attractive at the age of fifty!

Commenting on the incredibility and almost voyeuristic interest greeting sexuality in older women, Paula Weideger (1982) compared the films *Gigi* and *Harold and Maude*, as examples of the different social constructions of sexuality in middle-aged men and middle-aged women reflected in the media. Both films deal with the sexual attraction of an older person to a younger person, and with the subsequent attitudes of society. However, in *Gigi*, the older man openly dotes on the younger woman, in marked contrast to the reprobation which greets the older woman Maude, when her liaison with the younger Harold is made public. This reflects society's distaste at the thought of a sexually-active older woman, especially with a younger man. A woman such as Joan Collins, who can flaunt her sexuality and make a fortune out of it, represents the paradox which affects all menopausal women. Whilst we are reminded that youth and beauty are synonymous, and that the best thing the menopausal woman can do is disappear gracefully (as the menopausal 'media woman' does), we are simultaneously presented with the high media profile of a woman who has refused to do just that and is greatly rewarded for it. Of course, she has done it by looking young, conforming to social norms by defying the processes of ageing. The high profile of these celluloid women is almost a parody of the discourse which acts to constrain the majority of women, as they are defying the rules and almost revelling in being portrayed as wicked, i.e., 'bad'. This is an unreachable goal for the majority of women, who are more likely to identify with the woman in the 'before and after' advert for the latest wonder drug: tired, depressed and fading visibly, to be relieved by medical intervention which may only numb the pain and dull the senses but will provide an appearance of relief.

As women internalize these stereotypes we again experience a splitting between our own experience and the image of woman contained within the discourse. Thus many middle-aged women find themselves hiding or disguising their sexuality, for to express it would be to risk ridicule or revulsion. It is this that Weideger terms part of the 'menopausal disguise': women have to deny their own feelings, acting out a role which may not fit, which reinforces the sense of splitting between body and self. In her analysis of forty-five menopausal women, Itzen (1986) concluded:

Because of the extent to which we have internalised age–sex stereotypes we lead double lives. We live both our 'reality' and the 'reality' of the oppression. That is to say, we live what we know is true and we live the lie about us. We submit to the stereotypes and resist them simultaneously.

(Itzen 1986: 129)

Sue Condor (1986) called this process 'double consciousness': it applies to women's experiences of the mismatch between their own feelings and desires and the restrictions of the female role, throughout the whole life cycle. The prevailing discourse restricts women representing us solely or predominantly as reproducers, yet this restriction does not end when the potentiality of reproduction is no longer present. The menopause, the 'change', is not conceptualized as a period of release from the bonds of childbearing, as one might suppose it could be. It is seen as a period of depression, redundancy and uselessness, associated with anxiety, which provides further confirmation of the view that women are faulty vessels, needing to be controlled.

Life events

The discourse which positions menopausal women as redundant can only provide part of the explanation for the fact that some women experience psychological problems during this stage of the life cycle. There are many complex and interacting factors which determine whether an individual woman will experience difficulties, or be 'symptom free'. The internalization of the negative stereotypes and ideologies is just one influential factor.

One of the explanations which many professionals put forward to explain why some women experience psychological problems, in the form of depression or anxiety, during the menopause, is the experience of stressful life events. I discussed this argument in some detail when considering menstrual cycle problems (pp. 55–6) and the same issues arise here again. Without going into detail about the theoretical background to this debate, it is important to say that there is much evidence to suggest that many types of illness and psychological problems can be shown to be related to the occurrence of stressful life events (Brown and Harris 1978; Ganster and Victor 1988).

There seems to be evidence that stressful life events are more likely to influence a woman's menopausal symptoms than the biological event of cessation of menstruation, or the impact of ageing (Hunter 1987). Greene and Cooke (1980) report that stressful life events, which are related to psychological symptoms, tend to occur early in the menopause (age thirty-five to forty-five), generally before the hormonal changes discussed above have begun to take place. However, it has since been shown (Greene and Cooke 1982: quoted by Goudie 1986) that the occurrence of stressful life events is no greater for women during the menopause than during other phases of life. Thus it cannot be said that women suddenly experience an increase in stress which precipitates their symptoms. For although we may find a significant relationship between stress and illness at other times in the life cycle, the symptoms experienced by menopausal women do not necessarily result.

There may be an additive element involved in the relationship between psychological symptoms and life stress, with more severe life stress resulting in increases in symptoms. This would mean that women who have experienced stressful life events, such as bereavement, may be more vulnerable to psychological symptoms. However, these symptoms are likely to be interpreted as being menopausal, as a result of the attributional process which we have discussed above. Menopausal women will be conditioned to report certain types of symptoms, through the same process which ensures that certain symptoms are reported as being part of PMS or PND, attributing selective, negative experiences to internal pathology.

It is not only the psychological symptoms which will increase following a stressful life event, for it has been reported that somatic symptoms were greatest in one group of menopausal women when they had suffered a recent bereavement (Greene 1984). It is possible that the menopause itself may make women more vulnerable to stress (Greene 1984) in much the same way as the premenstrual phase of the menstrual cycle may be a vulnerable period for certain women, causing an exacerbation of negative attributions towards symptoms. Thus the experience of being menopausal may in itself be perceived as stressful, adding to any existing stresses to increase vulnerability. As many women seem to approach the menopause with trepidation and fear, it could suggest that these women are expecting it to be stressful in itself. However, this is a controversial theory: Resnick et al. (1984), in an open-ended interview of 145 women aged from thirty-six to seventy-five years, found that the menopause was not mentioned as a significant life event by any of the women. Goudie (1986) suggests that this finding is evidence of the fact that the menopause as a life event in itself 'is more readily supported by the women's doctors than by the women themselves'.

Thus the menopause is not necessarily a stressful time for all women. However, women who perceive themselves to be menopausal casualties, who present themselves as patients, may be more affected by life stresses, may perceive their lives to be more stressful, and for them the menopause may be a significant life event. Ballinger (1984) found that a group of menopausal 'patients' reported more stressful life events than a matched control group. However, it seemed that the patient group were reporting the same events as more distressing than the non-patient group, and were coping less effectively with stress. It is obviously very difficult to compare the subjective experiences of stress in any two people: we cannot say objectively how stressful the experience of any event should be. One could argue that it is the subjective experience of an event as stressful which is important, because it is this evaluation which will determine whether somatic or psychological symptoms will be associated with it. Thus there would seem to be two main conclusions which we could draw from this analysis of the relationship between stressful life events and menopausal symptoms:

1   that there is an additive factor at work, with an accumulation of stressors resulting in an increase of symptomatology during the menopause, as at other stages in the life cycle, with the added possibility that the menopause itself is being perceived as a stressor.

2   that women who present themselves as menopausal patients may be evaluating their lives as being more stressful than women who do not, regardless of the actual number of stressors which are present. Therefore, although life stress is an issue, it is not the presence of stress *per se* which is important, but the evaluation of it.

A stress management approach may go some of the way to alleviating menopausal problems for these women: teaching coping skills and providing women with accurate expectations of what they may experience. We would thus avoid an attribution of symptomatology to individual pathology: acknowledging psycho-social factors in women's lives.

The power of attitudes

That women should blame the menopause for physical and psychological problems suggests a highly negative attitude towards this phase in the life cycle. This is not surprising given the way in which menopausal women are both conceptualized and treated. That attitudes towards the body and towards reproduction can affect the experience of discomfort and of negative symptoms has already been discussed with relation to the menstrual cycle, in Chapter 3. One reason for examining these attitudes has been to attempt to distinguish between those women who experience severe discomfort, and present as 'patients' during the menopause, and those who report that they are experiencing no problems. Goudie (1986) reported that women who presented as patients have more negative attitudes than those who do not, in the dimensions of unpredictability, symptom control and external continuity. Goudie suggests that lack of symptom control is related to inadequate knowledge about the menopause, as well as being related to low self-esteem, 'which leads to a sense of hopelessness in the face of adversity'. The patient group felt that they had completely changed — both physically and in terms of their personalities — with the onset of menopause, viewing their symptoms as some sort of mystery over which they had little control.

Are these negative attitudes a universal phenomenon? A systematic study of this question by Neurgarten *et al.* (1963) found that 49 per cent of a cross-section of women held very negative attitudes towards the menopause, believing that it was unpleasant and restricting. The interesting finding was that the older women, who had experienced the menopause, had much more positive attitudes than the younger premenopausal women. This suggests that the actual experience of the menopause may not always justify women's negative expectations. This is a similar finding to that of Brooks-Gunn and Ruble (1982) who reported much more negative attitudes towards menstruation in premenarchal girls and young boys than in postmenarchal girls. Again, the group who had actual experience of menstruation were saying that it was not as bad as they had often been led to expect. A further interesting finding was that when the women in Neurgarten *et al.*'s study were asked to make a comparison between themselves and 'women in menopause', they all rated themselves as having less problems than other women. Neurgarten *et al.* argued that this was a defence mechanism, reflecting a deep-rooted ambivalence towards the menopause, which was a result of cultural attitudes towards ageing and femininity.

Fiona Goudie (1986) used the same assessment tool as used in the Neurgarten study above, which allowed her to carry out an analysis of attitude changes over a twenty-year period. What emerged was that *more* negative attitudes towards the menopause were expressed by the women in the 1986 study, despite the widening of opportunities and social roles for women over the past two decades, which might have been expected to produce more positive attitudes. Goudie suggests that this negative shift is evidence that women are becoming victims of the prolific advertising and media images in general which portray menopausal women in such a negative light. As HRT and the idea of the menopause as a deficiency syndrome were both absent in the early 1960s, it is possible that both have played an important role in producing more negative attitudes towards the menopause, reflected in the sample of women in Goudie's study.

Yet the different results obtained in the two studies discussed above may have been due to cultural differences, for it has been shown that women from different cultural backgrounds have very different attitudes towards the menopause. In one such study, Moaz *et al.* (1970) found that 60 per cent of European women, compared to 43 per cent of Oriental–Arab women, conceptualized the menopause in a negative way. The latter group saw the inability to have more children as the main negative factor at this stage of life: in contrast to the European women who reported worries about family, personality, and general social changes contributing towards their negative conceptualization of this stage of life. The worries which the women associated with the menopause are obviously dependent on the different social constructions of this phase of life in the two cultures. Women's individual worries will reflect the general views held in each society. The obvious connection here is that the attitudes and worries expressed by the women will be reflected in their experiences of symptomatology.

One study which examined the experiences of women from different cultural groups (Bart 1971) found that Jewish women experienced the highest rates of depression during the menopausal years. It suggested that this was because the traditional Jewish mother tends to identify closely with her children, and thus suffers from feelings of desertion and emptiness when they leave. Black women, who tended to play an active role in the upbringing of their grandchildren and who were much more likely to be employed outside the home, suffered the least from depression in this study. An intervening variable, which may compound or confound cultural factors, is that of socio-economic status, as low socio-economic status has been found to be associated with more negative attitudes towards the menopause in further studies (Eisner and Kelly 1980; Dege and Gretzinger 1982), as well as negative symptoms (Hunter *et al.* 1986). However, this may be related to whether or not women are employed outside the home, for there seems to be strong evidence to suggest that, in all cultures, women who were working outside the home reported lower rates of menopausal symptomatology, particularly after their children left home (Bart 1971; Hunter 1987). This may be because these women do not rely solely on their maternal role for their identity and self-esteem, in addition to the fact that women who are unemployed at any stage in the life cycle report higher rates of depression than those in paid employment (Brown and Harris 1978), as is the case with men. Bart also reported that women who lived in societies where a woman's status is enhanced with increasing age reported no menopausal depression.

These studies provide further support for the argument that negative menopausal experiences are largely socially constructed. If in societies where older women are valued (such as China) menopausal problems are nonexistent (Thompson 1971), we must conclude that women in Western society are being affected by the negative definition of our experience. If the menopause were seen to be a positive phase of the life cycle, a time for celebration of past achievements, less problems would occur. For if we compare our experience of ageing to that of women in China, ours is sadly lacking:

By the time her sons were mature and she was widowed, a Chinese woman was likely to be a lao-nien. . . . Hers was almost the only situation in which a woman could really shake off male domination and assume domination over males without incurring definite social disapproval. Moreover, any attempt to 'put her in her place', save in extreme cases, would probably have been socially disapproved.

(Levy 1948: 16)

The same phenomena can be observed in traditional Japanese society, in which older women are the most venerated age group, triumphant in their status and celebrated by the community (Embree 1946).

One would not wish to hold any society wherein women were severely restricted for a large part of their lives as a shining example for our own to emulate. However, as Weideger (1982) notes, 'the example of these cultures demonstrates that it is the cultural attitudes toward older women, not the biological realities of menopause, that are responsible for the meaning attached to menopause and aging'.

Mourning the empty nest: fact or fiction?

The evidence that women whose lives are centred on childbearing suffer from greater psychological symptoms during the menopause may suggest that the 'empty nest syndrome' is in operation, with women mourning their 'lost' children. It would seem that those women who have fully internalized the belief that femininity equals fecundity, and have devoted themselves to being mothers, are the most likely to suffer when the role is played out. It seems to be accepted in popular consciousness that women who have no employment outside the home, and who look to their role as mother for their identity, may suffer a crisis at this time. These women will have to concentrate on their 'sense of self' as the centre of definition (Rubin 1979) for perhaps the first time since adolescence. It is often a frightening prospect.

> I felt lost and aimless, walking around an empty house, still shopping for four when only the two of us were left. I look at myself in the mirror and wonder what it was all for. Who am I? A once a month mother when the children come to visit, the rest of the time just spent waiting.

> (P., aged 52)

It has been suggested by Gilligan and Murphy (1979) that women generally look to their relationships, their caring capacities, for their achievements and successes, whereas men look to their careers. As many of these relationships are changing during the middle years of a woman's life, a sense of loss may be experienced. Women look to their relationships for identity as they have been encouraged to do, and if they have no other role the loss will be greater. In addition, one of the most salient features of the menopause is the loss of the old self, which creates a period of transition for the woman, comparable to other transitional periods such as adolescence or marriage (Notman 1979). We have seen how a sense of loss is a feature of the transition to motherhood: a loss of the old self which the woman needs to mourn. A study of women who were psychiatric patients reinforced the importance of loss in women's lives, reporting that loss and change during times of transition — including the menopause — was associated with many of their problems (Scarf 1980). Notman suggests that the need to mourn is greater in this stage of life because the older woman has less choice in replacing what is lost. Women who have been taught to see their appearance and their sexuality as their main asset and the core of their identity may well experience a crisis of confidence as it seems to be stripped from them.

One of the losses which appears to be an influential factor in determining menopausal symptomatology, as we saw above, is the loss of children when they leave home. However, this 'empty nest syndrome' is not inevitable or universal; there is evidence that a majority of women experience an improvement in their lives after their children leave home (Deutcher 1968; Campbell 1976; Lowenthal 1975), being freed from many of the mundane tasks of childbearing. Neurgarten (1979) found no evidence for the empty nest syndrome, suggesting rather that a crisis will occur if the children *do not* leave home when they are expected to! This has been reported that many women anticipate their last child leaving with a sense of relief, rather than a sense of crisis (Lowenthal 1975) and that women whose children have left the nest are generally happier than a matched age group whose children are still at home (Glen 1975). In addition, many women experience a revitalization of their relationship with their partner as they enter a new phase of life:

> as you get to the end of it you feel as if it's the start of a new phase of life. My daughter will leave home, my husband and I can go places that we want to go without the ties of small children.
>
> (Goudie 1986: 55)

> There's not so much physical labour. There's not so much cooking and there's not so much mending, and, well, I remarked not long ago that for the first time since I can remember my evenings are free. And we had to be very economical to get the three children through college. We're over that hurdle now; we've completed it. Last fall was the first time in 27 years that I haven't gotten a child ready to go to school. That was very relaxing.
>
> (Deutcher 1968: 265)

Conversely, there is also a peak in the divorce statistics for this age group which can be interpreted in many ways. One obvious hypothesis is that many couples stay together to fulfil their roles as parents, and then find that they have little in common when the children have left home. As the majority of divorce petitions are submitted by women, it would seem that it is the women who resolve their dissatisfaction with the relationship by striving for a new life, a new role. One could argue that women are looking for new horizons during their menopausal years, looking for new ways of defining themselves. Discovering a new sense of self can be a positive experience, shedding the menstrual taboo can allow women to define themselves in ways other than as childrearers.

These changes have been seen as a part of changes taking place in midlife: not solely related to the biological changes of the meno-pause, as some 'experts' would have us believe. Researchers who have examined the development changes through the lifespan have suggested that women and men go through a predictable sequence of changes in midlife, changes which are different for men and women. Gutmann (1979) suggested that women 'become more aggressive in later life, less affiliative and more managerial or political', whilst men change in the 'reverse direction' becoming increasingly dependent on their wives. These developmental changes must contribute towards the high divorce rate in this age group, as women change from being affiliative to being more independent. It seems that some women look outwards, perhaps changing their whole lives during the menopause, taking advantage of the freedom which may be present for the first time since puberty. Other women look inwards and perhaps for the first time ever become depressed with these 'developmental changes leading to anxiety and development of somatic and psychological changes' (Goudie 1986).

Yet this group are in the minority. The majority of women whose children have left home seem to be happier and suffer less from depression than women with young children (Radloff 1979). The latter group, caring for their young offspring, actually suffer from higher rates of depression than any other single group in the popu-lation. Yet ironically these women are the group who should be experiencing total fulfilment if the myth of motherhood is to be believed. The deception is cruel.

The best years of our lives?

[the menopause is] the best form of birth control. Face it graciously and brag about it. It's great.
(Questionnaire respondant, Weideger 1982: 5)

So *can* the middle years in a woman's life be the best years, as the adage suggests? Can the menopause be welcomed as a new beginning: a crisis of identity which can be resolved through the forging of new roles, renewed independence? I have talked about the 'double consciousness' affecting menopausal women: implying that the reality of women's experience of sexuality and competency may be vastly different from the way they are positioned in the discourse. So what is the reality behind the image of the asexual, middle-aged woman? Are all women destined to a life of celibacy once they reach the menopause?

Helen Kaplan obviously thought not:

> Whilst some women report a decrease in sexual desire, many women actually feel an increase in erotic appetite during the menopausal years. Again, the fate of libido seems to depend on a constellation of factors which occur during this period, including physiological changes, sexual opportunity and diminution of inhibition. From a purely physiologic standpoint, libido should actually increase at menopause, because the woman's androgen, which is not materially affected by menopause, is now unopposed by estrogen. Indeed some women do behave in this manner, especially if they are not depressed *and can find interesting and interested partners*. (my emphasis)
>
> (Kaplan 1974: 111)

It is often the presence or absence of an interested or interesting partner which will determine the expression of a woman's sexuality, particularly for those women in heterosexual relationships. For as Ruth Herschberger points out: 'at menopause a husband often curtails sexual relations entirely, begs his wife to have breakfast in bed, and worst of all, professes an eternal love for her spirit no matter how withered her ovaries are' (Herschberger 1948: 58).

Yet women can still experience sexual desire and sexual satisfaction even though they are no longer fertile, a fact which is known to most women, even though they may not proclaim it openly. It has been suggested that the absence of fear of pregnancy, combined with a new sense of independence and power, can result in women feeling *more* sexual.

I am enjoying sex more in my forties than I did in my thirties; I enjoyed it more in my thirties than in my twenties. There's a liberating combination of experience, self-knowledge, and confidence, and an absence of pregnancy fears.

(Hite 1981: 509)

our sex life was much better after the children left home: no more worrying that they might hear us, or that we should be doing other things with them. It was as if we had suddenly been given back some of our youth!

(M. aged 59)

An interesting study (Bird 1979) claimed that menopausal women in their forties were a lot happier in the 1970s than they were in the 1950s. The researchers compared the results of a 1954 study investigating mental health in an American town — which reported that 21 per cent of the women in the forty to forty-nine age group were psychologically impaired — with a 1974 study in which only 8 per cent of women in the same age group were impaired. A cross-sectional study carried out in the USA in the mid-1970s (Williams 1983) produced similar results, showing that women who were in their forties in the 1970s were less likely to report psychological problems than their counterparts in the 1960s. It is suggested that this difference is due to the greater opportunities open to women, who 'may now take a new lease on life by pursuing educational and work-related goals, thus enriching the second half of life'.

This trend may seem to contradict the findings of Fiona Goudie (see p. 123) that attitudes were more negative in a group of women in the 1980s when compared to a 1970s study which used the same assessment methods. As I have said earlier, it is possible that this is a cross-cultural difference, between the 1980s British sample and the 1970s US sample, or the result of historical differences between the 1980s and 1970s. Also, Goudie's work was looking at attitudes, whereas the two studies above were looking at reported problems. Thus, the different results may be a result of the fact that negative attitudes alone do not inevitably result in depression; life events, social support, expectation, and availability of alternative roles and outlets during the menopausal years are important factors, as are changes in prevailing ideologies, with attitudes being one contributory factor.

In a review of the psychological research on the menopause,

Cooke (1984) acknowledges that care should pass from the hands of the gynaecologist and the general practitioners. However, he suggests that it should pass into the hands of other professional groups, thus perpetuating and reinforcing the disease model within which women's experiences are framed. Although Cooke is one of the few authors published in mainstream psychology texts at present who acknowledges that more 'radical changes at the macro-social level' are necessary if women are to be freed from menopausal distress, he still unfortunately concludes that there is very little empirical evidence to suggest that these changes will affect the level of disorder experienced by women. It is not surprising that there is little 'empirical' evidence, as cases where macro-social changes have taken place are few and far between and are unlikely to be documented in a systematic and 'empirical' way. This is further illustration of the problem which surfaces in any discussion of the psychology of women, where empirical 'objective' data are seen as a necessary prerequisite for any intervention or change. We have seen the evident need for macro- and micro-social changes in the analysis of the construction of the discourse which positions menopausal women, as well as from the reports of the women themselves.

The propagation of hormone replacement therapy locates a woman's problems within herself in a deterministic manner, through an analysis of her biological functioning. This is exactly the same process we have seen operating with PMS and PND: describing a menopausal deficiency disease means that a third syndrome exists to explain unhappiness and discontent in older women: a syndrome which is again rooted in women's reproductive biology. The few physical fluctuations which may be a result of hormonal changes are seen as being the major component of any reported distress. All the concomitant psychological and identity changes taking place during the menopause which are not hormonally mediated are seen as being of secondary importance, or ignored. Physical treatments mask the need for an analysis of the social and political contexts of older women's lives, and of the dominant beliefs and discourses which define and confine their existence.

It is not as a result of faulty hormones or faulty pathology that women are anxious or depressed during menopause. Locating moods in internal pathology only perpetuates the association between deviance, reproduction, and female sexuality: reinforcing the negative representations of the female body. It is a consequence of the narrow range of life choices and opportunities open to the majority of women that they are forced to seek definition predominantly through their sexuality and reproductive capacity, and are thus condemned to worthlessness after the onset of the menopause. By positioning menopausal women as useless, 'past it' in all senses, we are creating a situation in which depression is a probable result. It is not an immutable process: if women are valued for more than their reproductive capacity, they will not be seen, or see themselves, as redundant at forty. Many women have looked outside their reproductive role and found meaning in life which is not restricted by biology.

There is also a positive side to the menopause, as we have seen. Many women report positive experiences during this phase of life and in the years following. A new lease of life, a new identity, freedom from the ties of mothering, are just a few of the experiences quoted. This shows that women themselves can challenge the ideology and reframe their own lives, against the odds. We need to publicize the fact that life does not end at forty, so that younger women do not approach these years with dread. We need to challenge the stereotypes which define women as useless when their reproductive function is ended. Ageist and sexist stereotypes in the media, which reinforce the negative images of older women, must be continuously criticized and challenged. Positive images of older women, realistic and positive role models, must replace those which are currently available and which do so much damage.

Conclusion

Witches, wicked women, or patients: women confined

> The chains removed from the insane by Pinel were reattached by
> the great psychiatric nosologists. To be sure, the new chains con-
> formed to modern hygienic and humanitarian standards: they
> were not made of iron, but of words; their ostensible aim was not
> to imprison, but to cure.
>
> (Szasz 1973: 212)

Throughout this book I have argued that the discourses surrounding the female body and the reproductive cycle have been used to
confine women, to define women as dangerous and deviant, and to
exclude them from a role in society equal to that enjoyed by men.
The influence of the female body on the consciousness or
behaviour of women has either been exaggerated (in a negative
way) or denied, thereby preventing women from integrating their
bodies with their conceptualizations of self, and ultimately producing fragmented and split identities.

The way in which the association between wickedness, badness,
or infirmity and the female body has been institutionalized and
legitimated has differed from country to country, and from one
point in history to another. In the Middle Ages, wicked women
with power who challenged authority were designated witches, their
sexuality and their female bodies being seen as a central part of
their crime. The diagnosis or accusation of being a witch was
enough to dismiss a woman from society and even to condemn her
to death for daring to challenge the orthodox nature of a repressive
society, for practising medicine which challenged the accepted

practices of the legitimate doctors (frequently charlatans), or merely for being a woman.

The Victorians used a slightly more subtle way of dismissing and incarcerating women, always maintaining the association between the female body and wickedness or insanity. They elevated the connection between the womb and the brain to a scientific status, which decreed women unfit for anything other than childrearing, and certainly unfit for any role which might prove them to rival men. As I discussed earlier, hysteria became the accepted diagnosis for the female infirmity which resulted from women's invisible incarceration in the prison house of femininity, and hysterical women were sent to the asylum or confined to their sick beds at home.

In the twentieth century we bind women with the chains of nosology, pathologizing unhappiness as a disease, which we offer to cure with a multitude of psychotropic drugs. This psychiatric, or psychological, diagnosis acts to depoliticize women's behaviour and experiences. The concept of mental illness, and the consequent pathologizing of certain behaviours, has become the heir to witch-hunts as a means of social control and is used to classify and dismiss the behaviour of those who do not conform. It is no coincidence that the large majority of witches were women, as are the majority of those who receive psychiatric classification, women condemned to incarceration or 'treatment' for daring to challenge the orthodox practice of their patriarchal societies: 'Witch-hunts attempt to eliminate women who live outside the patriarchal family, who subvert a masculine version of society' (Daly 1978, quoted in Kramarae and Treichler 1985: 489).

Mental illness . . . for women [is] often a form of logical resistance to a 'kind and benevolent enemy' they are not permitted to openly fight. In a sick society, women who have difficulty fitting in are not ill but demonstrating a healthy positive response.

(Charlotte Perkins Gilman; quoted by Spender 1982: 377)

We do not burn our modern day 'witches', those women who receive a scientific diagnosis of mental illness to explain their rebellion or discontent; instead we silence them with psychotropic drugs, contain them in secure hospitals, or engage them in therapy aimed at improving their adaptation and dampening their rebellion.

Women who rebel or challenge their lot and who do not conform with the expectations of society are today more likely to be defined as ill than evil or criminal, as would previously have been the case. Yet the use of labels of illness, which are based on the positivistic philosophy of medical science, rather than the labels of badness or evil, based on a theological philosophy, still define women as separate, perpetuating the archetype of woman as deviant, and second rate. Szasz (1973) called this the 'rhetoric of rejection', the use of stigmatizing labels to exclude certain people from the mainstream of society. Many women are excluded from equal participation in society through a variety of labels and, as we have seen, many of these labels and classifications are related to the body, and specifically the reproductive cycle.

Thus, psychiatric classification associated with the female body cannot be separated from its social context, as it is used as a means of control to reinforce the power of those who determine the legitimacy of the 'diagnosis', and define certain behaviours or feelings as deviant, even illegitimate. I have tried to show how the discourse of reproduction has been used to legitimate the dismissal of women's unhappiness and distress in a biologically deterministic way: yet depression in women is largely rooted in the social construction of the female psyche, and in the necessity of living with the contradictions and expectations of being a woman in our society. Despite evidence to support this view (Brown and Harris 1978; Nairne and Smith 1984; Nicolson 1988), it is still maintained that women's depression is predominantly a result of hormonal factors of chemical imbalances. What Katrina Dalton, the guru of the medical model for reproductive madness, says about postnatal depression is as frequently said about the depressions that women experience at other stages of the life cycle:

The presentation of the PND has always been a psychiatric disease. They say the woman is mentally disturbed because she has to share herself with the baby and husband. But really it is a hormonally induced state. One day we will recognize that *all* depressions are caused by chemical disorders and imbalances. (my emphasis)

(Dalton, quoted by Dix 1986: 22)

If depression can be related to a stage in the reproductive life cycle — to menarche, menstruation, pregnancy or the menopause

— this only serves to perpetuate the pathological models of explanation for women's distress. The use of any psychological diagnosis defines a woman's identity: defines her as ill, as deviant, as needing help and assistance, and removes power and control from the individual woman. Throughout this book we have seen how the different stages in the reproductive life cycle are associated with diagnostic classifications which perpetuate this process.

It is partly the horror and fear which society associates with the female body, with female sexuality, which has provided the momentum for the classification and treatment of women for many centuries. It has been powerfully suggested that witchhunts have always been based on a fear of women's sexuality:

> The suggestion that the witchcraft craze was in large part a result of male paranoia about female sexuality gains considerable support from the words of Malleus Maleficarum (i.e., Hammer against witches). This document was published in 1486 by two Dominican inquisitors, with the authorization of Pope Innocent VIII, and it became the witchhunter's bible during the height of the Inquisition. The Malleus ascribes the preponderance of female witches to women's excessive sexuality.
>
> (Warren 1980: 490)

Is it a coincidence that modern theories and systems of control of women are located in the female body, related to a woman's sexuality, to her reproductive cycle? The fear of sexuality and power in sixteenth-century women which led to their labelling as witches parallels the fear of sexuality in the menstruating, pregnant or menopausal women today. This leads to splitting and denial and the diagnosis of 'syndromes' to dismiss any irregularities. The dichotomy in which the female body is simultaneously seen as attractive/seductive and horrifying/dangerous maintains women's separation of body and self.

The modern-day diagnostic categories of premenstrual syndrome, postnatal depression and the menopausal syndrome have assumed the legitimacy accorded 'scientific' theories, as they are part of a system of psychiatric classification which purports to explain the deviant behaviour of women. Women who complain of distress, of anger, of excessive libido; women who feel disenchanted following childbirth; women who feel disillusioned in their middle years can all be labelled ill, and so excluded and dismissed.

Yet there is no validity in using the term 'syndrome' to describe all distress experienced during the menstrual cycle, pregnancy or the menopause, as we have seen. As catch-all descriptions of distress, PMS, PND, or 'the menopause' are as meaningless as the use of hysteria to describe the unhappiness of the Victorian woman. The perpetuation of these syndromes in both scientific texts and popular consciousness says more about the way in which women are defined as useless, and the way in which classification is used as a means of social control, than it does about the present status of scientific knowledge.

This is not the first time that scientific classification has been used to legitimate convenient explanations for women's distress, elevating previously spurious theories based on the womb or female sexuality to a higher, scientific status. Jacqueline Rose, in her analysis of the role of Freudian theories in the maintenance of feminity, mentions how Charcot, in Paris, provided a background for Freud's writings on hysteria:

> Freud was working under Charcot whose first contribution to the study of hysteria was to move it out of the category of sexual malingering and into that of a specific and accredited neurological disease. The problem with Charcot's work is that while he was constructing the symptomatology of the disease (turning it into a respected object of the medical institution), he was reinforcing it as a special category of behaviour, visible to the eye, and the result of a degenerate hereditary position.
>
> (Rose 1986: 96)

Freud questioned the existence of hysteria as an identifiable and independent clinical entity which could be used to describe the behaviour of certain socially isolated or confined women. As the women who were described as hysterical were usually non-procreative, believed to be over-educated, or seen as innately perverted and diseased, the clinical label was undoubtedly a means of social control. Freud attempted to penetrate the surface of the disorder defined as hysteria, and to examine what the symptons were actually saying, rather than using the term hysteria simply as a descriptive term (Rose 1986).

This is what I am attempting to do with PMS, PND, and the menopausal deficiency syndrome: not merely examining the legitimacy of these as descriptive categories but trying to ascertain what the particular symptoms actually mean; why they occur in any individual woman. In his analysis of hysteria Freud used his theories of the unconscious to examine the meaning behind symptoms. I am not advocating this: I do not feel that within the context of this book I could do justice to a psychoanalytic interpretation of these syndromes, or of women's symptoms associated with the body. But it is important to recognize that the use of clinical classification to control women is not new, and neither is criticism of it. In fact this criticism goes back to Freud.

Throughout the book I have argued that there is little evidence for the idea that women are ruled by their hormones and therefore likely to be unbalanced — mad or bad — during particular stages of the reproductive cycle. What we have seen is that diagnostic categories have been used to define women as ill; to invoke the power of the specialist to provide a cure and thus controlling women whilst subjugating them. Yet there is still a need for us to acknowledge the importance of these different reproductive stages in the woman's life cycle; acknowledge that menarche, menstruation, pregnancy, and the menopause can have a profound effect on women's lives, on women's identity and conceptualization of self. However, we have seen that it is largely the social construction of these stages which at present produces the negative effects. To place women's experience of these states within a socio-political context is not to deny their existence but to shift the frame of reference, as well as the options for a feasible intervention.

To position women purely in terms of their reproductive status is to deny their autonomy, to deny them the possibility of self-actualization. We have seen how, within the present discourse concerning women, reproduction plays an insidious role in maintaining subordination: it defines woman through her womb, through her body, through the presence or absence of a child, the presence or absence of menstruation, the presence or absence of attractiveness, and sexuality.

Psychological research which confines itself to the examination of 'problems', to the establishment of objectively definable syndromes, is disabled and blinkered by its taken-for-granted ideological basis and acts to maintain the subordination of women as it further enfeebles them. Yet the dissection of this psychological research has supported my argument that women are *not* inevitably confined by their reproductive role and that it can be reconstructed as a positive aspect of female identity. For if it is social constructions of reproductive stages which largely render them damaging and frightening for women, a reconstruction can redress the balance, conceptualizing reproduction as a natural, positive aspect of female experience which belongs to women. Without the myths and the rhetoric, women may have more realistic expectations of the effects of menstruation, pregnancy and the menopause, and be able to travel through these life stages without having to reconcile their own experience with the contradictions inherent in present conceptualizations of femininity.

I have tried to go some way towards deconstructing the privileged position of science itself, through examining the way in which so-called objective, quantitative research provides a biased version of women's experiences, and generally omits a vital source of material: women's own discourse. I am not attempting to substitute one ideology for another, by declaring that the analysis of a different type of data will provide the 'truth', or even that a deconstruction of the present framework of understanding can provide a complete substitute explanation for women's distress. I do, however, hope that the analysis may point towards a more meaningful and enabling framework for understanding women's behaviour and women's experiences than those currently available within the scientific paradigm.

Symptoms and splitting

That the different stages of the reproductive cycle may be associated with particular stresses has been argued throughout the book; stresses which may increase the likelihood of any individual woman experiencing a sense of unhappiness. As this unhappiness does not easily fit into the social construction of femininity, except as part of an illness, women are isolated and 'split' from our own experiences. The mourning over the loss of self which may occur at the transitional stages of menarche, pregnancy, and the menopause should be an adaptive part of a changing identity, not be pathologized as a syndrome. Thus women's unhappiness or sadness, perhaps even depression, may be an adaptive reaction to change and totally understandable given the social constructions of reproduction and the female body. If women were to expect some sadness, some sense of loss, and were legitimately allowed to express discontent, they might not accept the pathological explanations so readily, and perhaps escape from the metaphorical chains of diagnosis.

Throughout this book I have examined the splitting between the woman and herself: the splitting in the adolescent, who cannot assimilate the changes in her developing body and thus separates them from herself; the splitting in the pregnant woman who is faced with the dichotomy of sexuality and motherhood, within the archetype of woman as mother; the splitting of the menopausal woman who cannot reconcile the archetype of uselessness and redundancy with her own experiences. Within psychoanalytic theories, and particularly object relations theories, splitting is a central component:

> Splitting represents the first attempt to organise the chaotic contents of the psyche and hence is fundamental to processes of ordinary thought and discrimination; more psychodynamically, it allows a separation to occur between good and bad parts of the psyche and of objects, thus preserving the existence of the good parts from the threatening, destructive fury of the bad and enhancing the security of the ego.

> (Frosh 1987: 122)

It is not possible to examine this theoretical argument in more detail within this book: suffice to say that splitting can be associated with particular stages in the development of the women's identity and in her journey through the life cycle. This splitting is not always negative, for some degree of splitting is always necessary as a means of coping with strains and contradictions which otherwise might engulf the self. Yet if women are always to be split, as a result of present constructions of their bodies and their sexuality, they will always be disabled by them.

Social constructionism — denying the existence of despair?

To deconstruct the syndromes associated with the menstrual cycle, pregnancy, and the menopause is not to deny the existence of unhappiness in individual women. To state that we have been subject to 'interior colonization' is not to say that the depression is not real. What this theoretical standpoint does suggest is that women are not *inevitably* depressed at any stage of their reproductive cycle, and that real explanations for depression are more likely to be found outside the woman: in her individual life situation or in the discourse which positions all women, rather than in her internal pathology, our 'raging hormones'. We need to reconceptualize these phenomena, PMS, PND, and the menopausal syndrome, to see them predominantly as expressions of women's struggles with our environment, as natural reactions to our position within the discourse which frames experience.

What of the individual woman who seeks help? A feminist approach to therapy — underpinned by a theory of gender and in which 'treatment' is not solely concerned with helping the woman adjust to her environment — may be far more appropriate than medication. Self-help groups and assertiveness training can provide women with support and encouragement; sharing experiences will reduce isolation and demonstrate that distress is not abnormal or evidence of sickness. If women need to use any form of medication to ease physical problems it will be more successful as part of a whole, positive approach, in which psychological and social needs are also addressed.

Suggesting therapy does not imply that women are ill, that they need to be treated. It does imply that there are many difficulties and contradictions inherent in being a woman in our society and that women may need support and understanding on an individual level. Yet in the advocation of therapy, we must be careful not to fall into the trap of maintaining women's oppression, for as Szasz notes:

> Rulers have always conspired against their subjects and sought to keep them in bondage; and to achieve their aims they have always relied on force or fraud. Indeed, when the justificatory rhetoric with which the oppressor conceals and mis-represents his true aims and methods is most effective — as had been the case formerly with tyranny justified by theology, and is the case with tyranny justified by therapy — the oppressor succeeds not only in subduing his victim but also of robbing him [sic] of a vocabulary for articulating his victimisation, thus making him a captive, deprived of all means of escape.

(Szasz 1973: 5)

We must not use therapy to justify the tyranny over women. Instead, it can be used to provide women with a voice to speak out against the stereotypes and challenge the dominant ideology. It can encourage women to see the female body in a positive light, not as a cross to bear. Women's individual problems can be addressed in therapy and individual coping skills devised, using an approach which does not pathologize the woman. To remove the chains of the reproductive syndromes we must remove the chains of the nosologists, who label and redefine our experiences.

Yet this does not dismiss the need for analysis and change on a wider, socio-cultural basis in order to challenge the ideologies of reproduction, as well as address the myriad problems associated with the experience of being a woman in our society. We need to acknowledge that change must take place at both an individual and a societal level before women can be free of their reproductive chains. As Elaine Showalter concluded in *The Female Malady*: 'Until women break them for themselves, the chains that make madness a female malady, like Blake's "mind-forged manacles", will simply forge themselves anew' (Showalter 1987: 250). The suggestion that psychology can offer anything which will further this breaking of the chains of reproduction may seem an anathema to many women. Yet a psychology of women, for women, can use the voices of women ourselves, piece together the different parts of our lives, to help towards the realization that, although we are often burdened with the definitions of womanhood which position us in order to constrain and control us, *we* can take control, change the definitions, and move towards a positive image of self. Psychology, within a feminist framework, can contribute to our knowledge about ourselves, our bodies, and our reproductive abilities, leading to the possibility of our reclaiming them with new power.

Notes

Chapter 2

1 Toxic Shock Syndrome is a rare but serious disease which mainly strikes menstruating women under thirty years old. Though the number of women is small, a few have died. TSS, which first came to public attention in 1980, is a syndrome, or group of symptoms. At present, only those people who have all the symptoms listed are officially counted as having TSS; others may have milder forms of the disease. The symptoms are a high fever (usually over 102°), vomiting, diarrhoea, a sudden drop in blood pressure which can lead to shock, and a sunburn-like rash.

The acronym TSS has also come to stand for Tough Shit Sweetie: both in protest at the lack of research on the safety of tampons and other 'feminine' products and as a comment on the often cavalier attitude of corporations and government agencies toward women's health issues.

(Kramarae and Treichler 1985: 455)

Chapter 3

1 There are many excellent reviews of the biochemical treatments of PMS (Janowsky *et al.* 1971; Culberg 1972; Tonks 1975; Steiner and Carroll 1977; Smith 1975; Bardwick 1976; Abplanalp 1983).
2 Increases in negative mood premenstrually (reported as increases in anxiety, restlessness, tension or irritability): Benedek and Rubinstein 1939; Beaumont *et al.* 1975; Garling and Roberts 1980; Golub 1976; Ivey and Bardwick 1968; Kirsten *et al.* 1981; Moos 1969; Parlee 1980; Patkai *et al.* 1974; Silbergeld *et al.* 1971; Silverman *et al.* 1974; Taylor 1979; Tiffany 1964; Voda 1980.
3 Reports of greatest increases in anxiety in the menstrual phase of the cycle: Beaumont *et al.* 1975; Englander-Golden *et al.* 1978; Golub and Harrington 1981; Parlee 1980; Stocker 1974; Wilcoxen *et al.* 1976.
4 No consistent variation in mood throughout the menstrual cycle: Kyger and Webb 1972; May 1976; Abplanalp 1979; Parlee 1980; Golub and Harrington 1981; Lahmeyer *et al.* 1982; O'Neil *et al.* 1984.

5 The most commonly used Moos Menstrual Distress Questionnaire (MDQ) has only five items which could be deemed positive out of a total of forty-eight, yet when positive items are included most women report high incidences of positive mood at all cycle stages, including the premenstrual or menstrual phases which are traditionally seen as periods of anxiety or depression. In my own research, a positive cluster of items was added to the existing negative clusters of the MDQ, and women reported feeling happy, elated, and generally positive about themselves throughout the whole cycle — there was no decrease premenstrually. In a study by Brooks *et al.* (1977) which examined menstrual attitudes, 77 per cent of subjects reported positive feelings towards menstruation, without denying its effects. So it would seem that if women were given the opportunity to report positive experiences, a different picture could emerge.

6 Positive moods in the premenstrual phase of the cycle: May 1976; Wetzel *et al.* 1975; McClure *et al.* 1971; Ederlyi 1962; Morris and Udry 1970. Peaks of positive feelings are more frequently recorded in the ovulatory, or mid-cycle, phase of the cycle: Rossi and Rossi 1977; Bardwick 1976; Ivey and Bardwick 1968; McCance *et al.* 1937; Little and Zahn 1974; Moos 1969; Taylor 1979; Voda 1980.

7 It has been suggested that labelling questionnaires as 'Menstrual Distress Questionnaires' (MDQ) will produce cyclical effects, whilst non-specific mood questionnaires show no cyclical variations. Golub and Harrington (1981) found cyclical changes in mood when using the MDQ, which is clearly labelled as measuring menstrual cycle variations in mood, and no such pattern in mood inventories which were not specifically menstrually related. In contrast, Chernovetz *et al.* (1979) found that male and female subjects reported less distress when the inventory was labelled as related to menstruation. Conversely, in a study of twenty-four phobic women patients, Vila and Beech (1980) found that negative mood change was reported on menstrually related retrospective questionnaires but not on concurrent questionnaires with the purpose of the study disguised. Other studies have suggested that the labelling or not of questionnaires as relating to menstruation has little effect. Markum (1976) gave women retrospective MDQ, either with neutral or menstrually related instructions, and no difference was found between the two groups on symptom reporting. Taylor (1979) and Rogers and Harding (1981) support this view, with studies in which there were no differences between symptom reports on daily and retrospective questionnaires.

8 In an interesting study which suggested that state changes could have benefits for menstruating women, Rodin (1976) manipulated the attributions of aroused women and showed that those who had a pill attribution, or who were warned of the effects of arousal, performed more efficiently than women with no source of attribution. Those who complained of high negative menstrual symptomatology, and who, it was concluded, therefore had a source for their arousal as they would make menstrual cycle attributions, performed better than low symptom women. Rodin suggests that this may result in the performance of menstruating women being more predictable than that of men, or non-

menstruating women, as changes in state can be anticipated and compensated for.

9 A study carried out on women in Japanese factories (Kirihara 1932) reported some decrease in efficiency associated with the menstrual period, but there were widespread individual differences, which prevent generalization. A study carried out on women in an electro-mechanical factory in Kharkov (Gorkine and Brandis 1937) showed increased susceptibility to fatigue and increased work breaks during the menstrual period, but, in general, no effects on performance.

A study carried out on women's output in different industries in wartime Britain (Anderson 1941) reported no consistent menstrual phase effects on performance.

Redgrove (1971) investigated eight women laundry workers, over 25 complete menstrual cycles and found no effects of cycle phase on work performance. The results were also obtained from a study of nine punch-card operators and three typists, using a four phase division of the menstrual cycle (dividing each woman's cycle into four phases of equal length).

Smith (1950a) studied the work performance of women in an aircraft factory, a parachute factory and a clothing factory, during World War II. Independent ratings made by foremen, who were unaware of the purposes of the study were used. No significant cycle variations in performance were found. Slightly longer ratings were given in the premenstrual and menstrual phases, but these did not become significant. In a follow-up study, Smith (1950b) evaluated the quality and quantity of production, in relation to the menstrual cycle, over a period of 41 days. Using a dichotomous analysis (menstrual—nonmenstrual) and a four phase division, he found no variation in quality related to a cycle day. He found some evidence of lower production premenstrually on tasks which demanded a high level of mental ability. However, this was balanced out by a higher level of work menstrually.

Finally, a comprehensive study carried out by Sowton and Myers (1928), analysing the performance of women in industry during the menstrual cycle, showed no significant relationship between cycle phase and performance.

10 In a review of the research of athletic performance, Ederlyi (1962) reported that 42—48 per cent showed no change in performance during the menstrual phase, 13—15 per cent showed improved performance, and 33 per cent showed worse performance than their usual average. Ederlyi attributed any decreased efficiency to nervous and emotional factors rather than hormonal changes, declaring that women athletes suffer from feelings of inferiority which may prevent them from competing at their usual level of performance.

A study of twenty-seven female swimmers aged twelve to sixteen (Astrand et al. 1963), analysing self-perceived changes in performance over the menstrual cycle, found performance peaks at menstruation for 1 woman; during the week after menstruation for 7; during the week preceding menstruation for 3, and no variation over the cycle for 16.

All of the women competed if an event fell during the menstrual period, yet 20 out of the 27 did not normally train during menstruation. Astrand suggests that psychological factors may be responsible for any detrimental effect of menstruation on performance.

A study of sixty-six women athletes at the Tokyo Olympics by Zaharieva (1965) found 15 per cent reporting performance decrement premenstrually and 17 per cent reporting performance decrement during menstruation. Sixty-three per cent of the women felt that they could reach peak form in a competition during menstruation, whilst 26 per cent were uncertain, showing lack of self-confidence. There was a notable difference in the confidence of swimmers and volleyball players, with the latter group exhibiting more self-confidence than the former. Female swimmers were less likely than any other group of athletes to train during menstruation (Zaharieva 1965; Ederlyi 1962); in fact, Zaharieva found swimmers to be the largest group of athletes never to train during menstruation (33 per cent).

11 No relationship between scores on bi-weekly psychology tests and cycle phase, for 101 women students, was found by Sommer (1972). Each subject's cycle was divided into four phases, and, both between and within group, comparisons made. There was some evidence that women were more likely to show their lowest scores in the premenstrual and menstrual phases, when compared to the other stages of the cycle. A second study carried out to examine the relationship between performance on bi-weekly psychology tests and cycle phase, in 125 women (Bernstein 1977), controlled for scholastic ability and motivation, and found no relationship between menstruation and performance.

Walsh, Budtz-Olson, Leader and Cummins (1981) assessed the performance of 341 women students, on medical or paramedical examinations. The cycle of each woman was divided into four, and a difference score computed for each of the four phases against the average of other examinations taken: thus allowing each woman to serve as her own control. There was no effect of cycle phase on performance; no relationship between performance and menstrual symptoms; and no relationship between performance and neuroticism, as measured on Eysenck's personality questionnaire.

Olasov (1972) examined the intellectual performance of thirty-two school teachers, both during menstruation and at mid-cycle. No relationship was found between experience of symptoms and performance, and no relationship found between cycle phase and performance.

Bibliography

Abplanalp, Judith M. (1979) 'Psychoendocrinology of the menstrual cycle: 11, The relationship between enjoyment of activities, moods and reproductive hormones', *Psychosomatic Medicine* 41(8): 605–15.

Abplanalp, Judith M. (1983) 'Premenstrual syndrome: a selective review', *Women and Health* Sum-Fall 8(2–3): 107–23.

Abraham, S. and Hargrove, C. (1980) 'Effects of vitamin B6 on premenstrual symptomatology in women with premenstrual syndromes: a double blind crossover study', *Infertility* 3: 150–64.

Abraham, S., Mira, M., McNeil, D., Vizzard, J., Fraser, I., and Llewellyn-Jones, D. (1985) 'Changes in mood and physical symptoms during the menstrual cycle', in D. Yusof, J. McGuire, and L. Demers (eds) *Premenstrual Syndrome and Dysmenorrhea*, Urban Schwarzuberg.

Adams, C. and Laurikietis, R. (1976) *The Gender Trap: A Closer Look at Sex Roles*, London: Virago.

Anderson, A. and McPherson, A. (1984) *Women's Problems in General Practice*, Oxford: Oxford University Press.

Anderson, M. (1941) Some health aspects of putting women to work in war industries, in *Seventh annual meeting, Industrial Hygiene Foundation*, 165–69.

Asso, D. (1983) *The Real Menstrual Cycle*, London: John Wiley & Sons.

Asso, D. (1986) 'The relationship between cyclical variations and sex differences in performance', in H. Baker (ed.) *Sex Differences in Human Performance*, London: John Wiley & Sons.

Asso, D. and Braier, J. (1982) 'Changes with the menstrual cycle in psychophysiological and self report measures of activation', *Biological Psychology* 15: 95–107.

Astrand, P., Englestrom, L., Erikson, B., Karlberg, P., Nylander, I., Salton, B., and Thoren, C. (1963) 'Girl swimmers: with special reference to respiratory and circulatory respiration', *Acta Ped. Suppl.* 147: 1–75.

Backstrom, T. (1975) 'Correlation of symptoms in pre-menstrual tension to oestrogen and progesterone concentrations in blood plasma', *Neuropsychobiology* 1(2): 80–6.

Ballinger, S. E. (1984) 'A comparison of life stresses and symptomatology of menopause clinic patients and non-patients', Australia, University of Sydney, unpublished.

Bardwick, J. (1971) *The Psychology of Women*, New York: Harper & Row.

Bardwick, J. (1976) 'Psychological correlates of the menstrual cycle and oral contraceptive medication', in I. Sacha (ed.) *Hormones, Behaviour and Psychopathology*, London: Raven Press.

Bardwick, J. and Behran, S. (1967) 'Investigation into the effects of anxiety, sexual arousal and menstrual cycle phase on uterine contractions', *Psychosomatic Medicine* 24: 468–82.

Bart, P. (1971) 'Depression in middle-aged women', in V. Gornick and B. Moran (eds) *Women in Sexist Society*, New York: Basic Books.

Beaumont, P., Richards, D., and Gelder, M. (1975) 'A study of minor psychiatric and physical symptoms during the menstrual cycle', *British Journal of Psychiatry* 126: 431–4.

Becket, H. (1986) 'Cognitive developmental theory in the study of adolescent identity development', in S. Wilkinson (ed.) *Feminist Social Psychology*, Milton Keynes: Open University Press.

Belmaker, R., Murphy, D., Wyatt, R., and Loriaux, L. (1974) 'Human platelet monoamine oxidase changes during the menstrual cycle', *Archives of General Psychiatry* 31: 553–6.

Benedek, T. (1963) 'An investigation of the sexual cycle in women', *Archives of General Psychiatry* 8: 25–36.

Benedek, T. and Rubenstein, B. (1939) 'The correlation between ovarian activity and psychodynamic processes: menstrual cycle phase', *Psychosomatic Medicine* 1: 461–85.

Benedek-Jazmann, L. and Hearn-Sturtevart, M. (1976) 'Pre-menstrual tension and functional infertility: aetiology and treatment', *Lancet* 1: 1095–8.

Bennett, E. (1981) 'Coping in the puerperium: the reported experience of new mothers', *Journal of Psychosomatic Research* 25: 13–21.

Berger, J. (1972) *Ways of Seeing*, London: Viking.

Bernstein, B. (1977) 'Effects of menstruation on academic performance among college women', *Archives of Sexual Behaviour* 6(4): 289–96.

Bird, C. (1979) 'The best years of a woman's life', *Psychology Today* June: 20–6.

Blandford, G. (1871) *Insanity and its Treatments*, Philadelphia: Henry C. Lea.

Bloch, D. (1972) 'Sex education practice of mothers', *Journal of Sex Education and Therapy* 7: 7–12.

Breen, D. (1975) *The Birth of a First Child*, London: Tavistock.

Brooks, G., Ruble, D., and Clarke, C. (1977) 'College women's attitudes and expectations concerning menstrual related change', *Psychosomatic Medicine* 39: 288–98.

Brooks-Gunn, G. and Ruble, D. (1982) 'Developmental processes in the experience of menarche', in R. Baum and T. Singer (eds) *Handbook of Medical Psychology* Volume 2, Hillsdale, New Jersey: Erlbaum.

Broverman, I., Broverman, D., Clarkson, F., Rosenkrantz, P., and

Vogel, S. (1970) 'Sex role stereotypes and clinical judgments of mental illness', *Journal of Consulting and Clinical Psychology* 34: 1–7.

Brown, G. and Harris, T. (1978) *Social Origins of Depression*, London: Tavistock.

Brown, J. and Brown, M. (1976) 'Psychiatric disorders associated with the menopause', in R. Beard (ed.) *The Menopause*, Lancaster: MTP Press.

Brownmiller, S. (1975) *Against Our Will: Men, Women and Rape*, New York: Simon & Schuster.

Brownmiller, S. (1984) *Femininity*, New York: Lindon Press.

Brush, M. G. (1977) 'The possible mechanisms causing the premenstrual tension syndrome', *Current Medical Research and Opinion* 4 Suppl 4: 9–15.

Butt, W., Watts, J., and Holder, G. (1983) 'The biochemical background to the premenstrual syndrome', in R. Taylor (ed.) *Premenstrual Syndrome*, London: Medical News Tribune, 16–24.

Campbell, A. (1976) 'Subjective measures of well-being', *American Psychologist* 31: 117–24.

Campbell, J. (1972) *The Masks of God: Primitive Mythology*, New York: Viking (first published 1959).

Carter, A. (1986) *The Magic Toyshop*, London: Virago.

Chernovetz, M., Jones, W., and Hanson, R. (1979) 'Predictability, attentional focus, sex-role orientation and menstrual related stress', *Psychosomatic Medicine* 41: 383–91.

Chesler, P. (1972) *Women and Madness*, New York: Avon Books.

Chodorow, N. (1978) *The Reproduction of Mothering; Psychoanalysis and the Sociology of Gender*, Berkley: University of California Press.

Clare, A. (1983) 'Psychiatric and social aspects of premenstrual complaints', *Psychological Medicine Mono.* suppl 4: 58.

Clarke, A. E. and Ruble, D. N. (1978) 'Young adolescents' beliefs concerning menstruation', *Child Development* 49: 231–4.

Clarke, M. (1981) 'The rejection of psychological approaches to mental disorder in late nineteenth-century British psychiatry', in A. Scull (ed.) *Madhouses, Mad-doctors and Madness: the Social History of Psychiatry in the Victorian Era*, London: Athlone Press.

Cochrane, R. and Stopes-Roe, M. (1981) 'Women, marriage and employment', *British Journal of Psychiatry* 139: 373–81.

Comer, L. (1976) 'The myth of motherhood', *Spokesman Pamphlet* 21, quoted in C. Adams and R. Laurikietis, *The Gender Trap: A Closer Look at Sex Roles*, London: Virago, 1976, p. 113.

Comerci, G. (1981) 'Symptoms associated with menstruation', *Paediatric Clinics of North America* 29(i): 177–200.

Comfort, A. (1977) *A Good Age*, London: Mitchell Beazley.

Condon, J. (1987) 'Psychological and physical symptoms during pregnancy: a comparison of male and female expectant parents', *Journal of Infant and Reproductive Psychology* 5(4): 207–20.

Condor, S. (1986) 'Sex role beliefs and "traditional" women: feminist and intergroup perspectives', in S. Wilkinson (ed.) *Feminist Social Psychology*, Milton Keynes: Open University Press.

Contratto, S. (1980) 'Maternal sexuality and asexual motherhood', in C. Sampson and E. Person (eds) *Women, Sex and Sexuality*, Chicago: University of Chicago Press.

Cooke, D. J. (1980) 'The structure of depression found in the general population', *Psychological Medicine* 10: 455–63.

Cooke, D. J. (1984) 'Psychosocial aspects of the climacteric', in A. Broome and L. Wallace (eds) *Psychology and Gynecological Problems*, London: Tavistock.

Cooke, W. R. (1945) 'The differential psychology of American women', *American Journal of Obstetrics and Gynecology* 49: 457–92.

Coppen, A. and Kessel, N. (1963) 'Menstruation and personality', *British Journal of Psychiatry* 109: 711–21.

Cowie, C. and Lees, S. (1987) 'Slags or drags', in *Sexuality: a Reader*, London: Virago.

Cowie, H. (1970) 'A psychological approach to cyclical patterns in industrial accidents', unpublished MSc thesis, University of Birmingham.

Craig, G. M. (1980) 'The premenstrual syndrome and prostaglandin metabolism', *British Journal of Family Planning* 6: 74–7.

Crist, R. and Hickenlooper, G. (1978) 'Problems in adolescent sexuality', in M. Barnard, B. Clancy, and R. Frantz (eds) *Human Sexuality for Health Professionals* 177–90, Toronto: Saunders.

Cubis, J., Cowen, A., and Lewin, T. (1986) 'Sexual experience, attitudes and decision making in adolescent Australian females', paper presented at the Eighth International Congress of the International Society of Obstetrics and Gynaecology, Australia.

Culberg, J. (1972) 'Mood changes and menstrual symptoms with different gestagen–oestrogen combinations', *Acta Psych. Scand.* 236: 1–86.

Dalton, K. (1959) 'Menstruation and acute psychiatric illness', *British Medical Journal* 1: 148–9.

Dalton, K. (1960a) 'The effect of menstruation on schoolgirls' weekly work', *British Medical Journal* 1: 326–8.

Dalton, K. (1960b) 'Menstruation and accidents', *British Medical Journal* 2: 1425–6.

Dalton, K. (1964) 'The influence of menstruation on health and disease', *Proceedings of the Royal Society of Medicine* 57: 18–20.

Dalton, K. (1966) 'The influence of a mother's menstruation on her child', *Proceedings of the Royal Society of Medicine* 59: 1014.

Dalton, K. (1968) 'Menstruation and examinations', *Lancet* 11: 1386–8.

Dalton, K. (1969) *The Menstrual Cycle*, Harmondsworth: Penguin.

Dalton, K. (1981) *The Sunday Times*, 15 November 1981.

Daly, M. (1978) *Gyn/Ecology: The Metaethics of Radical Feminism*, Boston: Beacon Books.

Dan, A. J. (1980) 'Free-associative versus self-report measures of emotional change over the menstrual cycle', in A. Dan, E. Graham, and C. Beecher (eds) *The Menstrual Cycle* I, New York: Springer.

Danza, R. (1983) 'Menarche: its effects on mother–daughter and father–daughter interactions', in S. Golub (ed.) *Menarche* 99–105, Lexington MA: Lexington Books.

Darwin, C. (1896) *The Descent of Man and Selection in Relation to Sex*, New York: Appleton.

Dege, K. and Gretzinger, J. (1982) 'Attitudes of families toward menopause', in A. Voda, M. Dinnerstein, and S. O'Donnell (eds) *Changing Perspectives on Menopause*, Austin: University of Texas Press.

Delaney, J., Lupton, M., and Toth, E. (1976) *The Curse: a Cultural History of Menstruation*, New York: E. P. Dutton.

Dennerstein, L., Spencer-Gardener, C., Brown, J., Smith, M., and Burrows, G, (1982) 'Psychoendocrinology of premenstrual tension', in 'Premenstrual Syndrome' (proceedings of a workshop held by the Royal College of Obstetricians and Gynaecologists) London.

Deutch, H. (1944) *Psychology of Women*, New York: Grune & Stratton.

Deutcher, I. (1968) 'The quality of postparental life', in B. Neurgarten (ed.) *Middle Age and Aging*, Chicago: University of Chicago Press.

Dickson, A. (1986) *The Mirror Within*, London: Quartet.

Dinardo, P. (1974) 'Psychological correlates of the menstrual cycle' (Doctoral dissertation, University of St Louis).

Direx, M. (1869) *Women's Complete Guide to Health*, New York: Townsend & Adams.

Dix, C. (1986) *The New Mother Syndrome: Coping with Postnatal Stress and Depression*, London: Allen & Unwin.

Dowrick, S. (1980) 'Stephanie Dowrick', in S. Dowrick and S. Grundberg (eds) *Why Children?*, London: The Women's Press.

Dunbar, R. (1985) 'Stress is a good contraceptive', *New Scientist*, 17 January 1985: 16–18.

Dunnigan, M. (1983) 'The recognition and management of the fluid retention syndrome of women', in R. Taylor (ed.) *Premenstrual Syndrome*, Medical News Tribune, 25–32.

Edelmann, R. and Connolly, K. (1987) 'The counselling needs of infertile couples', *Journal of Infant and Reproductive Psychology* 5(2): 63–70.

Ederlyi, G. (1962) 'Gynaecological study of female athletes', *Journal of Sports and Medical Fitness* 2: 174–9.

Ehrenreich, B. and English, D. (1979) *For Her Own Good: 150 Years of Experts' Advice to Women*, London: Pluto Press.

Eichenbaum, L. and Orbach, S. (1983) *What Do Women Want?*, London: Fontana.

Eisner, H. and Kelly, L. (1980) 'Attitudes of women toward menopause' (paper presented at Gerontological Society meeting), San Diego, California.

Elliot, S. (1984) 'Pregnancy and after', in S. Rachman (ed.) *Contributions to Medical Psychology* 3: 93–116, Pergamon Press.

Elliot, S. (1987) Book review: C. Dix, *The New Mother Syndrome: Coping with Postnatal Stress and Depression*, *Journal of Infant and Reproductive Psychology* 5(4): 247–8.

Elliot, S., Rugg, A., Watson, J., and Brough, D. (1983) 'Mood changes during pregnancy and birth of a child', *British Journal of Clinical Psychology* 22: 295–308.

Elmhirst, S. (1980) 'The early stages of female psychosexual development:

a Klienien view', in M. Kulpatrick (ed.) *Woman's Sexual Development: Explorations of Inner Space*, New York: Plenum.

Embree, J. (1946) *A Japanese Village: Suye Maru*, London: Routledge & Kegan Paul.

Englander-Golden, P., Whitmore, M., and Dienstbier, R. (1978) 'Menstrual cycle as a focus of study and self-report of moods and behaviours', *Motivation and Emotion* 2: 75–86.

Erikson, E. (1968) 'Womanhood and the inner space', in *Identity, Youth and Crisis*, New York: Norton.

Ernster, V. (1975) 'American menstrual experiences', *Sex roles* 1(1): 3–13.

Fagin, L. (1981) *Unemployment and Health in Families*, London: Department of Health and Social Security.

Feldman, H. (1974) 'Change in marriage and parenthood: a methodological design', in E. Peck and J. Senderovitz (eds) *Pronatalism: The Myth of Mom and Apple Pie*, New York: Thomas V. Growell.

Ferguson, M. (1983) *Forever Feminine: Women's Magazines and the Cult of Femininity*, London: Heinemann.

Ford, C. and Beach, F. (1951) *Patterns of Sexual Behaviour*, New York: Harper Brothers.

Fox, G. (1980) 'Mother–daughter communication about sex', *Family Relations* 29: 347–52.

Frank, R. T. (1931) 'The normal causes of premenstrual tension', *Archives of Neurology and Psychiatry* 26: 1053–7.

Frazer, J. (1959) *The New Golden Bough*, T. Gaster (ed.), New York: New American Library.

Friedan, B. (1963) *The Feminine Mystique*, Harmondsworth: Penguin Books.

Fromm, M. (1967) 'Psychoanalytic considerations on abortion', in H. Rosen (ed.) *Abortion in America*, Boston: Beacon.

Frosh, S. (1987) *The Politics of Psychoanalysis*, London: Macmillan.

Ganster, D. and Victor, B. (1988) 'The impact of social support on mental and physical health', *British Journal of Medical Psychology*, March: 17–36.

Gant, P. and McDonough, P. (1981) 'Adolescent dysmenorrhea', *Paediatric Clinics of North America* 28(1): 347–52.

Garling, P. and Roberts, S. (1980) 'An investigation of cyclic distress among staff nurses', in A. Dan, E. Graham, and C. Beecher (eds) *The Menstrual Cycle* I, New York: Springer.

Giele, J. Z. (ed.) (1982) *Women in the Middle Years: Current Knowledge and Directions for Research and Policy*, New York: John Wiley & Sons.

Gilligan, C. (1977) 'In a different voice: women's conceptions of self and of morality', *Harvard Educational Review* 47(4): 481–517.

Gilligan, C. (1982) 'Adult development and women's development, arrangements for a marriage', in J. Z. Giele (ed.) *Women in the Middle Years: Current Knowledge and Directions for Research and Policy*, New York: John Wiley & Sons.

Gilligan, C. and Murphy, J. (1979) 'Development from adolescence to adulthood: the philosopher and the dilemma of the fact', in D. Kuhn (ed.) *New Directions for Child Development: Intellectual Development Beyond Childhood* V, San Francisco: Jossey-Bass.

Glass, G., Heninger, G., Lansky, M., and Talan, K. (1971) 'Psychiatric emergency related to the menstrual cycle', *American Journal of Psychiatry* 128: 705–11.

Glen, N. (1975) 'Psychological well-being in the post-parental stage, some evidence from national surveys', *Journal of Marriage and the Family* 37: 105–10.

Golden, J. (1984) 'You're just in menopause', *Canadian Women Studies* 5(3): 74–6.

Golub, S. (1976) 'The magnitude of premenstrual anxiety and depression', *Psychosomatic Medicine* 38: 4–11.

Golub, S. and Harrington, D. (1981) 'Premenstrual and menstrual mood changes in adolescent women', *Journal of Personality and Social Psychology* 41(5): 961–5.

Gorkine, Z. and Brandis, S. H. (1937) 'Certaines fonctions physiologiques et la capacité de travail de la femme en rapport avec la menstruation', *Vrach. delo* 20: 445–54 (French summary).

Goudie, F. (1986) 'Menopause and middle age: a study of attitudes, knowledge, life stress and experiences in climacteric women' (Unpublished MSc dissertation, University of Newcastle).

Gough, H. (1975) 'Personality factors related to reported severity of menstrual distress', *Journal of Abnormal Psychology* 84: 59–65.

Graham, C. (1980) 'Cognition as related to menstrual cycle phase and estrogen level', in A. Dan, E. Graham, and C. Beecher (eds) *The Menstrual Cycle* I, New York: Springer.

Graham, H. and Oakley, A. (1981) 'Competing ideologies of reproduction: medical and maternal perspectives on pregnancy', in H. Roberts (ed.) *Women, Health and Reproduction*, London: Routledge & Kegan Paul.

Green, R. (1978) 'Sexual identity of 37 children raised by homosexual or transsexual parents', *American Journal of Psychiatry* 135: 692–7.

Greene, G. (1963) 'A vote against motherhood', *Saturday Evening Post*, 12 January.

Greene, J. G. (1984) *The Social and Psychological Origins of the Climacteric Syndrome*, Aldershot: Gower.

Greene, J. G. and Cooke, D. J. (1980) 'Life stress and symptoms in the climacterum', *British Journal of Psychiatry* 136: 486–91.

Greene, R. and Dalton, K. (1953) 'The premenstrual syndrome', *British Medical Journal* 1: 1007–14.

Grossman, A., Gaillard, C., McCartney, P., Rees, L., and Besser, G. (1982) 'Opiate modulation of the pituitary adrenal axis: effects of stress and circadian rhythm', *Clinical Endocrinology* 17: 279–86.

Gruba, G. and Rohrbaugh, M. (1975) 'MMPI correlates of menstrual distress', *Psychosomatic Medicine* 37(3): 265–73.

Gunn, J. (1924) *Gunn's New Family Physician*, New York: Saalfield Publishing.

Gutmann, D. (1979) 'The cross-cultural perspective: notes toward a comparative psychology of aging', in J. E. Birren and K. E. Schaive (eds)

153

Handbook of Psychology of Aging, New York: Van Nostrand.

Halbreich, U. and Endicott, J. (1981) 'Possible involvement of endorphin withdrawal or imbalance in specific premenstrual syndromes and post-partum depression', *Medical Hypotheses* (7): 1045–58.

Halbreich, U. and Kas, D. (1977) 'Variations in the taylor MAS of women with the premenstrual syndrome', *Journal of Psychosomatic Research* 21: 391–3.

Harrison, W., Sharpe, L., and Endicott, J. (1985) 'Treatment of pre-menstrual symptoms', *General Hospital Psychiatry* 17(1): 54–65.

Haspels, A. (1983) 'Premenstrual syndrome — a view from the continent', in R. Taylor (ed.) *Premenstrual Syndrome*, London: Medical News Tribune, 76–81.

Hays, H. (1972) *The Dangerous Sex*, New York: Pocket Books.

Heiman, M. (1965) 'A psychoanalytic view of pregnancy', in J. Rovinsky and A. Guttman (eds) *Medical, Surgical and Gynaecological Complications of Pregnancy* (2nd ed), Baltimore: The Williams and Watkins Co., 450–81.

Henriques, J., Hollway, W., Urwin, C., Venn, C., and Walkerdine, V. (1984) *Changing the Subject*, London: Methuen.

Herschberger, R. (1948) *Adam's Rib*, New York: Pellegrini & Cudahy.

Herzberg, B., Johnson, A., Brown, F., and Beck, A. (1970) 'Self-rating scale for depression, oral contraceptives and premenstrual depression', *Lancet* 1: 775.

Hey, V. (1985) 'Getting away with murder: PMT and the press', in S. Laws, V. Hey, and A. Eagan (eds) *Seeing Red: The Politics of Pre-menstrual Tension*, London: Hutchinson.

Hite, S. (1981) *The Hite Report: A Nationwide Study of Female Sexuality*, New York: Dell.

Hodges, S. (1987) 'The psychology of menstruation: how heavy is heavy?' (paper presented at the Women in Psychology conference 11–12 July 1987, Brunel, London).

Hollway, W. (1984) 'Gender difference and the production of subjectivity', in J. Henriques, W. Hollway, C. Urwin, C. Venn, and V. Walkerdine *Changing the Subject*, London: Methuen.

Hopkins, J., Marcus, M., and Campbell, S. (1984) 'Postpartum depression: a critical review', *Psychological Bulletin* 82(2): 498–515.

Horrobin, D., Manku, M., Nassur, B., and Evered, D. (1973) 'Prolactin and fluid and electrolyte balance', in J. L. Pasteels and C. Robyn (eds) *Human Prolactin*, Exerpta Medica: Amsterdam.

Hull, M., Glazener, C., Kelly, N., Conway, D., Foster, P., Watt, E., and Desai, K. (1985) 'Population study of causes, treatment and outcome of infertility', *British Medical Journal* 291: 1693–7.

Hunt, H. (1987) 'Towards positive mental health for women' (paper presented at the Women in Psychology conference 11–12 July 1987, Brunel, London).

Hunter, M. (1987) 'A prospective study of the menopause in a non-clinic population' (paper presented at the BPS London conference 17 December 1987).

Hunter, M., Battersby, R., and Whitehead, M. (1986) 'Relationships between psychological symptoms, somatic complaints and menopausal status', *Maturitas* 8: 217–28.

Itzen, C. (1986) 'Media images of women: the social construction of ageism and sexism', in S. Wilkinson (ed.) *Feminist Social Psychology*, London: Open University Press, 119–35.

Ivey, M. and Bardwick, J. (1968) 'Patterns of affective fluctuation in the menstrual cycle', *Psychosomatic Medicine* 30: 336–45.

Jahoda, M. (1982) *Employment and Unemployment*, London: Cambridge University Press.

Jakubowicz, D. (1983) 'The significance of prostaglandins in the premenstrual syndrome', in R. Taylor (ed.) *Premenstrual Syndrome*, London: Medical News Tribune 50–6.

Janowsky, D., Berens, S., Davis, J., and Vanderbilt, U. (1973) 'Correlations between mood, weight and electrolytes during the menstrual cycle: arenin-alsoterone hypothesis of premenstrual tension', *Psychosomatic Medicine* 35(2): 143–54.

Janowsky, D., Fann, W., and Davis, J. (1971) 'Monoamines and ovarian hormone-linked sexual and emotional changes: a review', *Archives of Sexual Behaviour* 1: 205–18.

Jenkins, R. (1985) *Sex Differences in Psychiatric Morbidity*, Cambridge: Cambridge University Press Psychological Medicine Monograph, suppl. 7.

Kaplan, H. (1974) *The New Sex Therapy*, New York: Brunner/Mazel, p. 111.

Kendell, R., Rennie, D., Clarke, J., and Dean, C. (1981) 'The social and obstetric correlates of psychiatric admissions in the puerperium', *Psychological Medicine* 11: 341–50.

Kenny, M. (1983) *She*, 6 August.

Kerr, G. (1977) 'The management of the premenstrual syndrome', *Current Medical Research and Opinion* 4(suppl. 4): 29–34.

Kincey, J. and McFarlane, T. (1984) 'Psychological aspects of hysterectomy', in A. Broome and L. Wallace (eds) *Psychology and Gynaecological Problems*, London: Tavistock.

Kingston, B. (1980) *Lifting the Curse*, London: Ebury Press.

Kinsbourne, M. (1971) 'Cognitive deficit: experimental analysis', in J. McGaugh (ed.) *Psychobiology*, New York: Academic Press.

Kirihara, H. (1932) 'Functional periodicity', *Report of the Institute of Scientific Labour*, Kurasiki Japan, 1453.

Kirsten, L., Rosenberg, G., and Smith, H. (1981) 'Cognitive changes during the menstrual cycle', *International Journal of Psychiatry in Medicine* 10: 339–49.

Kitzinger, C. (1987) *The Social Construction of Lesbianism*, London: Sage.

Kitzinger, S. (1983) *Women's Experience of Sex*, London: Dorling Kindersley.

Kitzinger, S. (1987) 'Birth plans and the control of territory' (guest address at the Women in Psychology conference, Brunel, London 11–12 July 1987).

Kliaber, E., Broverman, D., Vodel, W., and Kobayashi, Y. (1974) 'Rhythms in plasma MAO activity, EEG, and behaviour during the menstrual cycle', in M. Ferin, F. Halberg, R. Richart, and R. Vande Wiele (eds) *Biorhythms and Human Reproduction*, New York: John Wiley & Sons.

Klein, J. and Litt, I. (1983) 'Menarche and dysmenorrhea', in J. Brooks-Gunn and A. Peterson (eds) *Girls at Puberty* (73–88), New York: Plenum.

Koeske, R. (1977) 'The interaction of social-cognitive and physiological factors in premenstrual emotionality' (unpublished doctoral dissertation, Carnegie Mellon University).

Koeske, R. (1980) 'Theoretical perspectives on menstrual cycle research: the relevance of attributional approaches for the perception and explanation of premenstrual emotionality', in A. J. Dan, E. Graham, and C. Beecher (eds) *The Menstrual Cycle* I, New York: Springer.

Kohlberg, L. (1966) 'Stage and sequence: the cognitive–developmental approach to socialisation', in D. Goslin (ed.) *The Handbook of Socialisation Theory and Research*, Chicago: Rand McNally.

Kramarae, C. and Treichler, P. (1985) *A Feminist Dictionary*, London: Pandora Press.

Kyger, K. and Webb, W. (1972) 'Prostesterone levels and psychological state in normal women', *American Journal of Obstetrics and Gynecology* 113: 759–62.

Lahmeyer, H., Miller, M., DeLeon-Jones, F. (1982) 'Anxiety and mood fluctuation during the normal menstrual cycle', *Psychosomatic Medicine* 44: 2.

Lamott, K. (1977) 'Why men and women think differently', *Horizon* 19(3): 41–5.

Lauritzen, C. and Muller, P. (1977) 'Pathology and involution of the genitals in the aging female', in J. Money and H. Musaph (eds) *Handbook of Sexology*, Holland: Biomedical Press.

Lawlor, C. and Davis, A. (1981) 'Primary dysmenorrhea: relationship to personality and attitudes in adolescent females', *Journal of Adolescent Health Care* 1: 208–12.

Laws, S. (1985) 'Who needs PMT? A feminist approach to the politics of premenstrual tension', in S. Laws, V. Hey, and A. Eagen, *Seeing Red: The Politics of Premenstrual Tension*, London: Hutchinson.

Laws, S., Hey, V., and Eagen, A. (1985) *Seeing Red: The Politics of Premenstrual Tension*, London: Hutchison.

Lees, P. (1965) 'The vulnerability to trauma of women in relation to periodic stress' (Abstract, *the Medical Commission on Accident Prevention*, second annual report).

Lees, S. (1983) 'How boys slag off girls', *New Society*, 13 October 1983.

Lennert, M. and Wilson, N. (eds) (1973) *A Woman's New World Dictionary*, Lomita, California: 51% Publications. (Pamphlet, special collections, Northwestern University Library, Evanston, Illinois.

Levine, L. and Doherty, B. (1952) *The Menopause*, New York: Random Books.

Levitt, E. and Lubin, B. (1967) 'Some personality factors associated with menstrual complaints and menstrual attitudes', *Journal of Psychosomatic Research* 11: 267–70.

Levy, M. J. (1948) *The Family Revolution in Modern China*, Cambridge, Massachusetts: Harvard University Press.

Lewis, S. (1987) 'The transition to parenthood in dual earner couples' (paper presented at the annual conference of the Society for Infant and Reproductive Psychology, Edinburgh).

Little, B. C. and Zahn, T. P. (1974) 'Changes in mood and autonomic functioning during the menstrual cycle', *Psychophysiology* 1974, 11: 579–80.

Lloyd, E. (1987) 'Combining careers: motherhood and paid employment' (paper presented at the Women in Psychology conference 11–12 July 1987, Brunel, London).

Lowenthal, M. (1975) 'Psychosocial variations along the adult life course: frontiers for research and policy', *The Gerontologist* 15: 6–12.

Lowenthal, M., Thurnher, M., and Chiriboga, D. (1975) *Four Stages of Life*, San Francisco: Jossey Bass.

Luggin, R., Bensted, L., Petersson, B., and Jacobsen, A. (1984) 'Acute psychiatric admission related to the menstrual cycle', *Acta Psychiatrica Scandinavia* 69(6): 461–5.

Lyttle, J. (1988) *City Limits*, 3 March 1988.

McCance, R., Luff, M., and Widdowson, E. (1937) 'Physical and emotional periodicity in women', *Journal of Hygiene* 37: 571–611.

McClure, J., Reich, T., and Wetzel, R. (1971) 'Premenstrual symptoms as an indicator of affective disorder', *British Journal of Psychiatry* 119: 527–8.

McConville, B. (1987) *Mad to be a Mother*, London: Century Hutchinson.

McKeever, P. (1984) 'The perpetuation of menstrual shame: implications and directions', *Women and Health* 9(4): 33–47.

McKeever, P. and Galloway, S. (1984) 'Effects of nongynaecological surgery on the regularity of the menstrual cycle', *Nursing Research* 33(1): 421–6.

McKinley, S. and McKinley, J. (1973) 'Selected studies of the menopause', *Journal of Biosocial Science* 5: 533–55.

MacKinnon, I., MacKinnon, P., and Thomson, P. (1959) 'Lethal hazards of the luteal phase of the menstrual cycle', *British Medical Journal* 1: 1015–17.

MacKinnon, L. (1983) 'Feminism, Marxism, method and the state: an agenda for theory', *Signs* 7(3): 514–44.

MacKinnon, P. and MacKinnon, I. (1956) 'Hazards of the menstrual cycle', *British Medical Journal* 1: 555.

Macy, C. (1986) 'Psychological factors in nausea and vomiting in pregnancy: a review', *Journal of Reproductive and Infant Psychology* 4(1–2): 23–56.

Mahlstedt, P. (1985) 'The psychosexual component of infertility', *Fertility and Sterility* 43: 335–46.

Maitland, S. (1981) *Daughter of Jerusalem*, London: Pavanne.

Mandell, A. and Mandell, J. (1967) 'Suicide and the menstrual cycle', *Journal of the American Medical Association* 200: 792–3.

Markum, R. (1976) 'Assessment of the reliability of and the effect of neutral instructions on the symptom ratings of the Moos Menstrual Questionnaire', *Psychosomatic Research* 38: 163–72.

Mattson, B. and von Schoultz, B. (1974) 'A comparison between lithium, placebo and a diuretic in premenstrual tension', *Acta Psychiatrica Scandinavia* Suppl. 255: 75–83.

Maudsley, H. (1874) 'Sex in mind and in education', *Fortnightly Review* 15: 466–83.

May, R. (1976) 'Mood shifts and the menstrual cycle', *Journal of Psychosomatic Research* 20: 125–30.

Millett, K. (1971) *Sexual Politics*, New York: Avon Books.

Moaz, B., Dowerty, N. Antonovsky, A., and Wijenbeek, H. (1970) 'Female attitudes to menopause', *Social Psychiatry* 5(1): 35–40.

Moos, R. H. (1969) 'Typology of menstrual cycle symptoms', *American Journal of Obstetrics and Gynecology* 103: 390–402 (a).

Moos, R. H. (1978) 'Toward a menstrual cycle symptom typology', *Journal of Psychosomatic Research* 22(1): 31–40.

Morris, N. and Udry, J. (1970) 'Variations in pedometer activity during the menstrual cycle', in *Obstetrics and Gynecology* 35: 199–201.

Morrison, A. (1848) *Outlines of Lectures on the Nature, Causes and Treatment of Insanity*, London: Longmans, Brown, Green & Longmans.

Morton, J., Additon, H., Addison, R., Hunt, L., and Sullivan, J. J. (1953) 'A clinical study of premenstrual tension', *American Journal of Obstetrics and Gynecology* 65: 1182–91.

Moss, P., Bolland, G., Foxman, R., and Owen, C. (1986) 'Marital relations during transition to parenthood', *Journal of Reproductive and Infant Psychology* 4(1–2): 57–68.

Moss, P., Bolland, G., Foxman, R., and Owen, C. (1987) 'The division of household work during the transition to parenthood', *Journal of Infant and Reproductive Psychology* 5(2): 71–86.

Moss, P. and Brannen, J. (1986) 'Daycare for children under two' (paper presented to the Annual Conference of the Association of Child Psychology and Psychiatry, London: June 1986).

Moss, Z. (1970) 'It hurts to be alive and obsolete; the aging woman', in R. Morgan (ed.) *Sisterhood is Powerful: An Anthology of Writings from the Women's Liberation Movement*, New York: Vintage.

Nadelson, C. (1980) 'Normal and special aspects of pregnancy: a psychological approach', in C. Nadelson and T. Nadelson (eds) *Pregnancy*, New York: Springer, p. 74.

Nairne, K. and Smith, G. (1984) *Coping with Depression*, London: The Women's Press.

Nathenson, C. and Lorenz, G. (1982) 'Women and health: the social dimensions of biomedical data', in J. Geile (ed.) *Women in the Middle Years*, New York: John Wiley & Sons.

Neurgarten, B. (1979) 'Time, age and the life cycle', *American Journal of Psychiatry* 136: 1887–94.

Neurgarten, B. and Kraines, R. (1965) 'Menopausal symptoms in women of various ages', *Psychosomatic Medicine* 27: 266.

Neurgarten, B., Wood, V., Kraines, R., and Loomis, B. (1963) 'Women's attitudes towards the menopause', *Vita Humana* 6: 140–51.

Newton, N. (1955) *Maternal Emotions*, New York: P. Hoeber.

Newton, N. (1973) 'Interrelationships between sexual responsiveness, birth and breastfeeding', in J. Zubin and J. Money (eds) *Contemporary Sexual Behaviour: Current Issues in the Seventies*, Baltimore: John Hopkins.

Nicolson, P. (1986) 'Developing a feminist approach to depression following childbirth', in S. Wilkinson (ed.) *Feminist Social Psychology*, Milton Keynes: Open University Press.

Nicolson, P. (1988) 'The social psychology of postnatal depression' (unpublished PhD thesis, London: University of London).

Notman, M. (1979) 'Midlife concerns of women: implications of the menopause', *American Journal of Psychiatry* 136(10): 1270–2173.

Notman, M. and Nadelson, C. (1979) 'Reproductive crises', in A. M. Brodsky and R. Hare-Mustin (eds) *Women and Psychotherapy*, New York: Guildford.

Novak, E. (1921) *Menstruation and its Disorders*, New York: Appleton & Company.

Oakley, A. (1975) 'The trap of medicalised motherhood', *New Society* 34: 639.

Oakley, A. (1979) 'The baby blues', *New Society*, April 1979.

Oakley, A. (1984) *Taking it Like a Woman*, London: Flamingo.

Oakley, A. (1986) *Telling the Truth about Jerusalem*, London: Blackwell.

O'Brien, P., Craven, D., and Selby, S. (1979) 'Treatment of premenstrual syndrome by spirolactone', *British Journal of Obstetrics and Gynaecology* 86: 142–7.

Olasov, J. (1972) 'Cyclic variation and intellectual performance in women' (Master's thesis, Cincinnati, Ohio: Xavier University).

O'Neil, M., Lancee, W., and Freeman, J. (1984) 'Fluctuations in psychological distress during the menstrual cycle', *Canadian Journal of Psychiatry* 29(5): 373–8.

Orbach, S. (1986) *Hunger Strike*, London: Faber & Faber.

Paige, K. (1973) 'Women learn to sing the menstrual blues', *Psychology Today* 7(4): 41–6.

Parlee, M. (1973) 'The premenstrual syndrome', *Psychological Bulletin* 80: 454–65.

Parlee, M. (1975) 'Menstruation and voluntary participation in a psychology experiment', in 'A new psychology of menstruation' (symposium presented at the 83rd annual meeting of the American Psychological Association, Chicago).

Parlee, M. (1980) 'Changes in mood and activation level during the menstrual cycle in experimentally naïve subjects', in A. J. Dan, E. Graham, and C. Beecher (eds) *The Menstrual Cycle* I, New York: Springer.

Parlee, M. (1981) 'Gaps in behavioural research on the menstrual cycle', in

P. Komneich, M. McSweeny, J. Noack, and N. Elder (eds) *The Menstrual Cycle* II, New York: Springer.

Pasten, L. (1978) *The Five Stages of Grief*, New York: Norton.

Paterson, M. E. L. (1985) *The Menopause*, London: Ebury Press.

Patkai, P., Johannson, G., and Post, B. (1974) 'Mood alertness and sympathetic-adrenal medullary activity during the menstrual cycle', *Psychosomatic Medicine* 36: 503–12.

Patkai, P. and Peterson, K. (1975) 'Psychophysiological correlates of premenstrual tension', in Reports from the Department of Psychology, University of Stockholm, 446: 16.

Penfold, S. and Walker, G. (1984) *Women and the Psychiatric Paradox*, Milton Keynes: Open University Press.

Perlmutter, E. and Bart, P. B. (1982) 'Changing views of "the change". A critical review and suggestions for an attributional approach', in A. Voda, M. Dinnerstein, and S. R. O'Donnell (eds) (1982) *Changing Perspectives on Menopause*, Austin, USA: University of Texas Press.

Plath, S. (1962) 'Childless woman', in S. Plath, *Collected Poems*, London: Faber & Faber.

Prill, H. (1978) 'Ueber das Klimakterium zur Physiologie und Pathologie der Altersvor Gaenge bei der Frau', *Zeitschrift Fuer Gerontologie* 11: 39–53.

Pryor, K. (1973) *Nursing Your Baby*, New York: Pocket Books.

Puolakka, J. and Makarainen, L. (1985) 6: keto-prostaglandin f loc and thoronboxane in premenstrual syndrome: the effect of treatment with prostaglandin synthesis premenstrually (unpublished manuscript). Cited in W. Harrison, L. Sharpe, and J. Endicott, 'Treatment of premenstrual symptoms', *General Hospital Psychiatry* 7: 54–65.

Radloff, L. (1979) 'Sex differences in depression: the effects of occupation and marital status', *Sex Roles* 1: 249–65.

Raval, H., Slade, P., Buck, P., and Lieberman, B. (1987) 'The impact of infertility on emotions and the marital and sexual relationship', *Journal of Infant and Reproductive Psychology* 5(4): 221–35.

Reading, A. (1983) *Psychological Aspects of Pregnancy*, Harlow: Longman.

Redgrove, J. (1971) 'Menstrual cycles' in W. Colquhoun (ed.) *Biological Rhythms and Human Performance*, London: Academic Press.

Rees, L. (1953) 'The premenstrual syndrome and its treatment', *British Medical Journal* 1: 1014–16.

Reid, R. and Yen, S. (1981) 'Premenstrual syndrome', *American Journal of Obstetrics and Gynecology* 109: 1036–41.

Reitz, R. (1981) *Menopause: A Positive Approach*, London: Unwin.

Resnick, J. L., Doughtery, R. N., and Notelovitz, N. (1984) 'Significant life events and sources of stress in healthy climacteric women' (paper presented at the Fourth International Conference on the Menopause, Buen a vista, Florida, October 1984).

Rich, A. (1986) *Of Woman Born*, London: Virago.

Rierden, J. and Koff, E. (1980) 'The psychological impact of menarche:

integrative vs disruptive changes', *Journal of Youth and Adolescence* 9(1): 49–58.

Roberts, H. (1981) 'Male hegemony in family planning', in H. Roberts (ed.) *Women, Health and Reproduction*, London: Routledge & Kegan Paul.

Roberts, T. and Burns, J. (1987) 'Women and mental handicap: the oppression of the normal' (paper presented at the Women in Psychology conference 11–12 July 1987, Brunel, London).

Robins, D. and Cohen, P. (1978) *Knuckle Sandwich*, Harmondsworth: Penguin.

Rodin, J. (1976) 'Menstruation, reattribution and competence', *Journal of Personality and Social Psychology* 33: 345–53.

Rogers, M. and Harding, S. (1981) 'Retrospective and daily measures in men and women', in P. Kommeneich, M. McSweeny, J. Noak, and S. Elder (eds) *The Menstrual Cycle II: Research & Implications for Women's Health*, New York: Springer.

Rose, D. (1969) 'Oral contraceptives and depression', *Lancet* ii: 321.

Rose, J. (1986) *Sexuality in the Field of Vision*, London: Verso.

Rosenbaum, M. (1979) 'The changing body image of the adolescent girl', in M. Sugar (ed.) *Female Adolescent Development*, Lexington, MA: Lexington Books.

Rossan, S. (1987a) 'Identity and its development in adulthood', in T. Honess and K. Yardley (eds) *Self and Identity: Perspectives Across the Life Span*, London: Routledge.

Rossan, S. (1987b) Unpublished case studies.

Rossi, A. (1973) 'Maternalism, sexuality and the new feminism', in J. Zubin and J. Money (eds) *Contemporary Sexual Behaviour: Current Issues in the Seventies*, Baltimore: John Hopkins Press.

Rossi, A. and Rossi, P. (1977) 'Body time and social time: mood patterns by menstrual cycle phase and day of the week', *Social Science Research* 6: 273–308.

Rubin, L. B. (1979) *Women of a Certain Age: the Midlife Search for Self*, New York: Harper & Row.

Ruble, D. (1977) 'Premenstrual symptoms: a reinterpretation', *Science* 197: 291–2.

Sampson, G. (1979) 'Premenstrual tension: a double-blind controlled trial of progesterone and placebo', *British Journal of Psychiatry* 135: 209–15.

Sayers, J. (1982) *Biological Politics: Feminist and Anti-feminist Perspectives*, London: Tavistock.

Sayers, J. (1988) 'Childbirth: patriarchal and maternal influences', unpublished manuscript.

Scarf, M. (1980) *Unfinished Business: Pressure Points in the Lives of Women*, New York: Doubleday.

Schacter, S. and Singer, J. (1962) 'Cognitive, social and physiological determinants of emotional states', *Psychological Review* 69: 379–99.

Schulz, M. (1975) 'The semantic derogation of women', in B. Thorne and N. Henley (eds) *Language and Sex: Difference and Dominance*, Rowley,

MA: Newley House, 64–75.

Scott-Hall, W. (1916) *Sexual Knowledge*, Philadelphia: J.C. Winston.

Scott-Palmer, J. and Skevington, S. (1981) 'Pain during childbirth and menstruation: a study of locus of control', *Journal of Psychosomatic Research* 25: 151–5.

Seward, G. H. (1944) 'Psychological effects of the menstrual cycle on women workers', *Psychological Bulletin* 41: 90–102.

Sharpe, S. (1981) *Just Like a Girl: How Girls Learn to be Women*, Harmondsworth: Penguin.

Shaw, D. (1983) 'Hormones, amines and mood', in R. Taylor (ed.) *Premenstrual Syndrome*, London: Medical New Tribune, 33–6.

Sheldrake, P. and Cormack, M. (1976) 'Variations in menstrual cycle symptom reporting', *Journal of Psychosomatic Research* 20: 169–77.

Shopper, M. (1979) 'The (Re) discovery of the vagina and the importance of the menstrual tampon', in M. Sugar (ed.) *Female Adolescent Development*, 214–33.

Showalter, E. (1987) *The Female Malady: Women, Madness and English Culture, 1830–1980*, London: Virago.

Shreeve, C. (1984) *The Premenstrual Syndrome*, Wellingborough: Thorsons.

Shuttle, P. and Redgrove, P. (1986) *The Wise Wound: Menstruation and Everywoman*, London: Paladin.

Siegal, J., Johnson, J., and Sarason, I. (1979) 'Life changes and menstrual discomfort', *Journal of Psychosomatic Medicine* 5, 1: 41–6.

Silbergeld, S., Brast, N., and Noble, E. (1971) 'The menstrual cycle: a double blind study of symptoms, mood and behaviour, and biochemical variables using envoid and placebo', *Psychosomatic Medicine* 33: 411–28.

Silverman, E., Zimmer, C., and Silverman, F. (1974) 'Variability of stutterers' disfluency: the menstrual cycle', *Perceptual and Motor Skills* 38: 1037–8.

Singer, K., Cheng, R., and Schou, M. (1974) 'A controlled evaluation of lithium in the premenstrual tension syndrome', *British Journal of Psychiatry* 124: 50–1.

Skey, F. (1867) *Hysteria* (Second edition), London: Longmans, Green, Reader and Dyer.

Slade, P. and Jenner, F. (1979) 'Autonomic activity in subjects reporting change in effect in the menstrual cycle', *British Journal of Social and Clinical Psychology* 18: 135–6.

Smart, R. (1963) 'The importance of negative results in psychological research', *The Canadian Psychologist* 5: 225–32.

Smith, A. (1950a) 'Menstruation and industrial efficiency I. Absenteeism and activity level', *Journal of Applied Psychology* 34: 1–5.

Smith, A. (1950b) 'Menstruation and industrial efficiency II. Quality and quantity of production', *Journal of Applied Psychology* 34: 148–52.

Smith, S. (1975) 'Mood and the menstrual cycle', in E. Sacher (ed.) *Topics in Psychoneuroendocrinology*, New York: Grune & Stratton.

Smith, W. Tyler (1848) 'The climacteric disease in women', 607. Quoted in Showalter E. (1987) *The Female Malady: Women, Madness and English Culture, 1830–1980*, London: Virago.

Smith-Rosenberg, C. (1972) 'The hysterical woman: sex roles in nineteenth-century America', *Social Research* 39: 652–78.

Smith-Rosenberg, C. and Rosenberg, C. (1973) 'The female animal: medical and biological views of woman and her role in nineteenth-century America', *Journal of American History* 60: 332–56.

Solberg, D., Butler, J., and Wagner, N. (1973) 'Sexual behaviour in pregnancy', *New England Medical Journal* 288: 1098–103.

Sommer, B. (1972) 'Menstrual cycle changes and intellectual performance', *Psychosomatic Medicine* 34: 263–9.

Sommer, B. (1983) 'How does menstruation affect cognitive competence and physiological response?', *Women and Health* 8(2–3): 53–90.

Sosa, R., Kennell, J., Klaus, M., Robertson, S., and Urrutia, J. (1980) 'The effect of a supportive companion on perinatal problems, length of labour and mother–infant interaction', *The New England Journal of Medicine* 303: 597–600.

Sowton, S. and Meyers, C. (1928) 'Two contributions to the experimental study of the menstrual cycle. I. Its influence on mental and muscular efficiency', *Industrial Fatigue Research Board* 45: 72.

Spanier, G. (1977) 'Sources of sex information and premarital sexual behaviour', *Journal of Sex Research* 13(2): 73–88.

Spencer, H. (1896) *The Principles of Biology*, New York: Appleton.

Spender, D. (1980) 'Disappearing tricks', in D. Spencer and E. Sarah (eds) *Learning to Lose: Sexism and Education*, London: The Women's Press.

Spender, D. (1982) *Women of Ideas and What Men Have Done to Them — From Aphra Benn to Adrienne Rich*, London: Routledge & Kegan Paul.

Spender, D. (1985) *Man-Made Language* (Second edition) London: Routledge & Kegan Paul.

Stadel, B. and Weiss, N. (1975) 'Characteristics of menopausal women: a survey of King and Pierce counties in Washington, 1973–1974', *American Journal of Epidemiology* 102: 206–16.

Steiner, M. (1979) 'Psychobiology of mental disorders associated with childbearing', *Acta Scandinavia* 60: 449–64.

Steiner, M. and Carroll, B. J. (1977) 'The psychobiology of premenstrual dysphoria: review of theories and treatments', *Psychoneuroendocrinology* 2, 4: 321–35.

Stewart, D., Raskin, J., Garfinkel, D., McDonald, O., and Robinson, E. (1987) 'Anorexia nervosa, bulimia and pregnancy' (paper presented at the annual conference of the Society for Reproductive and Infant Psychology, Edinburgh, 1987).

Stocker, J. (1974) 'Motor performance and state anxiety at selected stages of the menstrual cycle', *Dissertation Abstracts International* 34 7(A): 3971–872.

Swaffield, L. (1987) *Nursing Standard*, 21 November 1987.

Szasz, T. (1973) *Ideology and Insanity*, London: Calder & Boyers.

Taylor, J. (1979) 'The timing of menstruation related symptoms assessed by a daily symptom rating', *Acta Psychiatrica Scandinavia* 60: 87–105.

Taylor, R. (1983) 'The significance of treatment responses in determining the aetiology of the premenstrual syndrome', in R. Taylor (ed.) *Premenstrual Syndrome*, London: Medical News Tribune, 72–5.

Taylor, W. (1871) *A Physician's Counsel to Women in Health and Disease*, Springfield: W. Holland.

Thompson, C. (1971) *On Women*, New York: New American Library.

Tickner, L. (1987) 'The body politic: female sexuality and women artists since 1970', in R. Parker and G. Pollock (eds) *Framing Feminism: Art and the Women's Movement 1970–1985*, London: Pandora Press.

Tiffany, P. (1964) 'A tension inventory to reveal subjective changes accompanying the menstrual cycle', *Dissertation Abstracts International* 25: 2864–B.

Tilt, E. (1852) *The Elements of Health, and Principles of Feminine Hygiene*, London: Henry G. Bohen.

Tobin-Richards, M., Boxer, A., and Peterson, A. (1983) 'The psychological significance of pubertal change: sex differences in perceptions of self during early adolescence', in L. Brooks-Gunn and A. Peterson (eds) *Girls at Puberty*, New York: Plenum.

Tonks, C. (1975) 'Premenstrual tension in contemporary psychiatry', *British Journal of Psychiatry*, Special Publication 9: 399–408.

Tonks, C., Rack, P., and Rose, M. (1968) 'Attempted suicide and the menstrual cycle', *Journal of Psychosomatic Research* 11, 4: 319–23.

Tuch, R. (1975) 'The relationship between a mother's menstrual status and her response to illness in her child', *Psychosomatic Medicine* 37: 388–94.

Ussher, J. (1987) 'Variations in performance, mood and state during the menstrual cycle', unpublished PhD thesis, University of London.

Van den Akker, O. (1985) 'A psychophysiological investigation of menstrual cycle distress', unpublished PhD thesis, University of London.

Vance, C. (1984) *Pleasure and Danger: Exploring Female Sexuality*, London: Routledge & Kegan Paul.

Varma, T. (1983) 'Hormones and electrolytes in the premenstrual syndrome', in R. Taylor (ed.) *Premenstrual Syndrome*, London: Medical News Tribune, 60–2.

Vellay, P. (1986) 'Sexuality and pregnancy' (paper presented at the 8th International Congress of the International Society of Obstetrics and Gynaecology, Australia, 1986).

Vila, J. and Beech, H. (1980) 'Premenstrual symptomatology: an interaction hypothesis', *British Journal of Social and Clinical Psychology* 1980: 1973.

Voda, A. (1980) 'Pattern of progesterone and aldosterone in ovulating women during the menstrual cycle', in A. J. Dan, E. Graham, and C. Beecher (eds) *The Menstrual Cycle I*, New York: Springer.

Walsh, K. (1985) *Understanding Brain Damage*, Edinburgh: Churchill Livingstone.

Walsh, R., Budtz-Olsen, I., Leader, C., and Cummins, R. (1981) 'The menstrual cycle, personality and academic performance', *Archives of General Psychiatry* 38(2): 219–21.

Wandor, S. (1980) in S. Dowrick and S. Grundberg (eds) *Why Children?* London: The Women's Press, 133–43.

Warren, M. (1980) *The Nature of Women: An Encyclopedia and Guide to the Literature*, Inverness, California: Edgpress.

Weideger, P. (1982) *Female Cycles*, London: The Women's Press.

Welburn, V. (1980) *Postnatal Depression*, London: Fontana.

Wetzel, R. and McClure, J. (1972) 'Suicide and the menstrual cycle: a review', *Comprehensive Psychiatry* 13: 369–74.

Wetzel, R., Reich, T., McClure, J., and Wald, J. (1975) 'Premenstrual affective syndrome and affective disorder', in *British Journal of Psychiatry* 127: 219–22.

Whisnant, L. and Zegans, L. (1975) 'A study of attitudes towards menarche in white, middle-class America in adolescent girls', *American Journal of Psychiatry* 138: 809–14.

Whitehead, R. (1934) 'Women pilots', *Journal of Aviation Medicine* 5: 47–9.

Wilcoxen, L., Schrader, S., and Sherif, C. (1976) 'Daily self reports on activities, life events, moods, and somatic changes during the menstrual cycle', *Psychosomatic Medicine* 38(6): 399–417.

Wilkinson, S. (1986) *Feminist Social Psychology*, London: Open University Press.

Williams, L. (1983) 'Beliefs and attitudes of young girls regarding menstruation', in S. Golub (ed.) *Menarche* (139–48), Lexington, MA: Lexington Books.

Wilson, R. A. (1966) *Feminine Forever*, New York: Mayflower-Dell.

Windolz, G. (1987) 'The explicity-stated rationale for the involuntary commitment of the mentally ill given by the nineteenth-century German-speaking psychiatrists', *Psychological Medicine* 17: 291–5.

Winship, J. (1983) *Femininity and Women's Magazines*, Open University Course 'The changing experiences of women', Unit 6, Milton Keynes: Open University Press.

Winston, F. (1973) 'Oral contraceptives, pyridoxine and depression', *American Journal of Psychiatry* 130: 1217–21.

Wood, A. Douglas (1971) 'The fashionable diseases: women's complaints and their treatment in nineteenth-century America', in M. Hartman and L. Banner (eds) *Clio's Consciousness Raised*, New York: Harper & Row.

Wood, A. Douglas (1973) 'The fashionable diseases: women's complaints and their treatment in nineteenth-century America', *Journal of Interdisciplinary History* 4: 29.

Wood, C. and Jakubowicz, D. (1980) 'The treatment of premenstrual symptoms with mefenbamic acid', *British Journal of Obstetrics and Gynaecology* 87: 627–30.

Woods, N., Dery, M., and Most, E. (1982) 'Recollection of menarche, current menstrual attitude and peri-menstrual symptoms', *Psychosomatic Medicine* 44, 3: 285–97.

Woollett, A. (1987) 'Why motherhood is popular: an analysis of mothers' and childless women's accounts' (paper presented at the Women in Psychology conference 11–12 July 1987, Brunel, London).

World Health Organisation (1981) 'Scientific group research on menopause', *Technical Reports Series* 670, Geneva.

Zaharieva, E. (1965) 'Survey of sportswomen at the Tokyo Olympics', *Journal of Sports Medicine and Physical Fitness* 5: 215–19.

Zavalloni, M. (1973) 'Social identity perspectives and prospects', *Social Science Information* 12: 463–77.

Zimmerman, E. and Parlee, M. (1973) 'Behavioural changes associated with the menstrual cycle: an experimental investigation', *Journal of Applied Social Psychology* 3(4): 335–44.

Zola, I. (1966) 'Culture and symptoms: an analysis of patients' presenting symptoms', *American Sociological Review* 31: 615.

Name index

Subject index

academic performance 60
accidents 44, 51, 62
adolescence 21, 24, 30, 39, 80, 98
ageing 106, 116, 125
AIDS 15
anorexia nervosa 39, 99
anxiety 84, 91, 100, 120
archetypes 14, 18, 26, 62, 64, 68, 83, 101, 135
arousal 53, 54
athletic performance 59
attitudes 30, 50, 55, 116, 122, 130
attribution 53, 54, 115, 121, 122

baby blues 85, 86, 92
beauty 38, 99, 116
blood 39, 43, 44, 52, 107
biology 70, 87, 115
brain 2, 5
breast feeding 97
breasts 22, 97, 98

ceremonies 31, 33
children 66, 116, 127
chinese foot binding 33
circumcision 33
climacteric 106
clitoridectomy 6, 7, 110
cognitive 114, 115
contraception 114, 115
crime 51, 62, 67

defilement 43

depersonalization 77
depression 51, 54, 82, 84, 87, 88, 100, 110, 112, 120, 135, 139, 140
diagnosis 48–50, 67, 69, 72, 85–7, 110
divorce 127
dysmenorrhea 37

education 1–3, 10, 35, 61, 130
empiricism x, 42
employment 3, 89, 90, 130
empty nest syndrome 126, 127
experimental tests 60

femininity 33, 34, 50, 73, 79, 81, 101, 137, 139
feminist therapy 141
fertility 31, 104, 105, 107, 129
forceps 78
framing 17, 77, 106, 118

genitals 19–22, 35, 94
grieving 88

hormone replacement therapy 111–13, 123, 131
hormones xii, 42, 44, 48, 49, 87, 138
hysterectomy 113
hysteria 4, 5, 6, 51, 134, 137

ideal woman 38, 82

171